Padraic O'Farrell is the author of thirty books, one of which, *The Burning of Brinsley MacNamara,* is an elaboration of the first episode in this work. Other works include *Rebel Heart,* a novel about the life of Michael Collins, along with *Who's Who in the Irish War of Independence, The Blacksmith of Ballinalee, Superstitions of the Irish Country People, Green and Chaste and Foolish — Irish Literary and Theatrical Anecdotes* and many more. He is also a freelance journalist and contributes regularly to *The Irish Times* and *The Examiner.* He has adapted two of John B. Keane's books for the stage and his comedy scripts have been used by Maureen Potter, Anna Manahan, Maureen Toal and Eileen Colgan.

TALES FOR THE TELLING
TRUE LIFE STORIES OF
IRISH 'SCANDALS'

Padraic O'Farrell

The Collins Press

To Maureen
In appreciation of forty great years!

Published by The Collins Press, Carey's Lane, The Huguenot
Quarter, Cork

© Padraic O'Farrell

British Library Cataloguing in publication data.
A CIP catalogue record for this book is available from the British
Library.

Printed in Ireland by Colour Books Ltd., Dublin

Cover design by Upper Case Ltd., Cornmarket Street, Cork

ISBN 1-898256-16-0

CONTENTS

ACKNOWLEDGEMENTS

I wish to thank David Walton of Walton's Music Publishers for permission to quote 'The Battle of Baltinglass', Mercier Press for permission to use excerpts from Eric Cross' *The Tailor and Ansty*, Hugh Leonard for his *Sunday Independent* extract, the Oireachtas Library for permission to quote liberally from official Dáil and Senate Debate Reports and René Dardis and Anvil Books Ltd. for quotations from Seamus Brady's *Doctor of Millions*. Eugene McCartan, on behalf of the Irish Communist Party, kindly gave me permission to quote from *The Communist Party in Ireland: An Outline History* and the *Irish Workers' Voice*. I thank Ulick O'Connor for his kind assistance. I thank Des Guckian for his permission to quote from *The Gralton Affair 1886-1945*. I have attempted to trace Martin McGoldrick, author of the Gralton ballad, without success. I would welcome information of his whereabouts, so that I may thank him for it.

I thank the following for considerable assistance: Tony Cox and Carmel Heffernan, Westmeath County Library; Carmel Moore, Wicklow County Library; Sean Ó Súilleabháin, Leitrim County Library; Tim Cadogan, Cork County Library; Maeve Kane, Registrar, The High Court; Patrick Melvin and Maura Corcoran, Oireachtas Library; Dr Pat Donlon and Staff, National Library of Ireland, Phyllis Ryan and Carolyn Swift.

My daughter Aisling did Trojan work at the word-processor and my wife Maureen, as usual, proof-read with an eye for error like a scandal-monger's, but much prettier! Thanks to them and to my agent, Jonathan Williams, and editor, Maria O'Donovan of The Collins Press, who took on the job of publishing at short notice.

Sit up here till I tell you about every one of them. They are all great, but ...!

INTRODUCTION

According to Oscar Wilde, 'Scandal is gossip made tedious by morality'. While the 'scandals' in this book constitute more than whispers across garden fences, some of them were events that sent hypocrites or Pharisees rushing for holy clichés with which to defend self-righteous citadels of superior sanctity. Others would have been amusing were it not for the distress they caused their victims. All of them occurred when 'moral high ground' was Alpine and its fuglemen yodelled devotional incantations against all who did not conform. We are a nation proud of our heritage and our culture. It is right that it should be so. In the main, we are a Christian people. Yet in so many ways we have displayed a lack of Christian charity towards our neighbours, even some who considered themselves friends, that neutral observers would be forgiven for labelling us a cruel race, a people who revel in throwing muck and pulling down a successful colleague.

Some of the graft of the period in which the following events occurred survives. There is the odd 'cute hoor' who will try every low-down trick in the 'Gurriers' Manual of Artful Trickery' to further his own interests. Not alone will he knife his mother in the back to get what he wants, he will take out her ribs, sharpen them and go after his father, sisters and brothers. Because he has survived, he is more cunning, more vicious and more deadly in his calumny and in his deceit.

Also, there is still the person with very worthy ideals, but who resolutely refuses to see, let alone tolerate another's point of view. He fits into one of many categories of bigots. He shouts 'Scandal!' if there is the slightest deviation from his idea of what is right.

There are genuine 'scandals' too, many bearing the imprimatur of state approval: staggering fees and remunerations, fabrication of rules to accommodate interested parties, back-handers in business, in crime; even in sport?

The reader should not approach this book with a heavy heart, however. The 'scandals' outlined in the pages that follow caused no deaths and damaged more pockets than minds. If reputations suffered in some circles, they grew healthy in others. The very fact that some of the stories are categorised as 'scandals' may be their most dishonourable feature. In our quaint way of finding Irish solutions through neglect, some of them have never been resolved. When they are discussed, whatever the official verdict, the fire that hides behind the smoke flickers during good conversation and the snug lawyer finds some new evidence to support his particular point of view. He has met another woman who knows a man who was near the place when so-and-so did such-and-such, so the truth will out!

Good old Ireland! *Gradh mo Croidhe*! Sensation once again!

THE CASE OF THE SQUINTING WINDOWS

Delvin, Co. Westmeath, stands where the Mullingar road parts to reach towards the Meath towns of Navan and Kells. It is a one-street village and from one bay window near its centre the full streetscape may be viewed. Older inhabitants call this 'The Squinting Window', although they may object to their hinterland being called 'The Valley of the Squinting Windows'. One of their own, John Weldon, called it that. Under the pseudonym Brinsley MacNamara, he wrote a book and gave it that title. Its publication led to a furore. In Delvin initially, but later across literary Ireland, a controversy raged. It rankles to this day among some people. Yet it was not Brinsley MacNamara, but his father, James Weldon, who suffered most from the protracted episode.

James Weldon was a farmer's son from Ballinea, west of Mullingar. In 1883, he began his career as a national school-teacher in Killough, four miles south-east of Delvin. Six years later, he married a local girl, Fanny Duncan. Fanny gave birth to the couple's first child, a boy, on 6 September 1890. This lad, John Weldon, would grow up to become Brinsley MacNamara.

More children arrived and the family moved to the school residence at Ballinvalley, Delvin. Close by was the two-storey school where James became principal teacher. His eldest son left for Dublin in 1909, to study for the Civil Service. Visits to the Abbey Theatre made him aware that his future was in acting or writing. He joined the Abbey company in 1910, and adopted his pseudonym. He toured the United States in 1911.

Meanwhile, letters began arriving in the Department of Education, conveying complaints about James Weldon. One of them bore the names of eight people from Delvin. It transpired later that these signatures were forged. The letter claimed that James Weldon gave a man money to buy paraffin oil to burn a stack of hay and a hay-shifter belonging to a farmer called Casey. Weldon also wanted the man to shoot the former school principal, Mr Duffy, it alleged. Furthermore, he was 'drunk in the town every night [and] had a free fight in a public house and boxed through the yard in the presence of about 20 of his scholars'.

The Department wrote to the school manager, Fr Tuite, who defended his teacher. He told how James' wife Fanny had a miscarriage and how a youth named Growney had accused Weldon of 'kicking the belly out of her'. This incited his anger. He added a rumour that Weldon had squared Growney 'by a pecuniary consideration' into dropping an assault case. Fr Tuite named and criticised another enemy of Weldon's. Michael Merriman was, Tuite wrote, 'of an adventurous disposition and had a hand in every bit of mischief that happened in Delvin'. His grudge against Weldon came out of the teacher's refusal to falsify attendance registers in respect of Merriman's children, the parish priest wrote.

James Weldon had problems with more than his neighbours. His limbs pained because of a fall from a horse when he was younger. School inspectors came frequently and complained about various aspects of his work. This brought more stress, leading to further heavy drinking and outbursts of temper. The relationship between him and his eldest son was unhealthy too, since John relinquished his studies for the Civil Service. So when Brinsley MacNamara arrived home in Ballinvalley in 1913 after his Abbey tour, he received a cold welcome from his father. In the evenings he took the keys of the schoolhouse and spent hours there, writing by candlelight. His sister, Nellie, brought him tea and food. A novel was emerging and a publishing house, Maunsel and Company, was interested. Its managing director, George Roberts, was wary of possible libel in its chapters. A careful man, he had rejected James Joyce's *Dubliners* in 1914. Roberts questioned and requested alterations. In May 1918, Maunsel's published Brinsley MacNamara's *The*

Valley of the Squinting Windows, and Delvin was never the same again.

At first, the villagers were quite proud. Jack Weldon, a local, had written a book. Some far bigger towns had no author to call their own. Also, according to those who read the daily papers, the reviews were not too bad. Then someone in the village got a copy of the new novel. Some say that the reader was a woman and that she sat with an audience of laughing females on the steps of Clonyn Castle beside the town. Peals of laughter rang out as the listeners claimed that they recognised the local postmistress and the butcher and the dressmaker in the story. The layout of Garradrimna, the village in the book, coincided exactly with Delvin. Garradrimna's environs lay the same distances from the village and in the same directions as Delvin's. The book referred to 'The Valley' and Weldon lived in Ballinvalley.

Another account tells how James Clyne read from the novel to the patrons of his public house. Clyne also owned a butcher's shop next door. His mouth fell open when he read:

> There now was the butcher's stall, kept filthily, where she might buy her bits of beef or mutton occasionally. She caught a glimpse of the victualler standing with his dirty wife amid the strong-smelling meat. The name above the door was that of the public house beside it.

Garradrimna's butcher had a barren wife. The Clynes were childless. Soon the local dressmaker learned that a dressmaker in the book, just like her, had a 'spoiled priest' in the family. Delvin's postmistress lived in the precise spot as her counterpart in 'The Valley' who steamed open letters. Hackney-car owners, farmers, and assorted tradesmen thought Jack Weldon had taken liberties too. Only the reviled schoolteacher, James Weldon, could have informed his son of one sordid aspect of the book's plot, many claimed. It concerned the killing of an infant born out of wedlock many years before. Added to the existing unpopularity of James Weldon, this was too much for most of Delvin's community.

Whether events in Clyne's pub on the evening of 28 May 1918 were as dramatic as folklore tells, is of little importance. Indeed, there is some evidence to suggest that meetings about the book were taking place before that and that letters of complaint were reaching newspaper editors who published articles by MacNamara. A libel action may have been in the offing.

A Royal Irish Constabulary (RIC) patrol present in Delvin was heavier than would be normal for the funeral which took place on that Tuesday evening. The deceased was popular and a considerable crowd congregated at the church and later at Clyne's pub. There was drinking and intense discussion indoors as Ballinvalley schoolmaster James Weldon stopped to chat to saddlemaker Thomas North on the footpath outside North's shop, a few yards away. John Weldon (Brinsley MacNamara) was inside. The pair soon noticed a mob gathering and moving towards them. Some say James Weldon took on the mob, but proved no match for it. Others say that he and North withdrew into the house to warn John Weldon whom we will call Brinsley MacNamara from this point on.

MacNamara escaped through the back of the house and ran to Martinstown Hall, a mile and a half away. The Delvin Volunteers were drilling there. The mob followed, but by the time they reached the hall, their prey was running across country to his uncle's home in Ballinea, 14 miles away. They called on the Volunteers to support them in placing a picket on Ballinvalley school the next day. Then they returned to Delvin, borrowed two motor cycles and took turns scouring the countryside looking for Brinsley. The *Westmeath Examiner* of 22 June 1918 described what happened back at North's:

When the crowd came up ... Corcoran and Clyne, who were the leaders of that particular mob, began to shout, 'Let us drive him out' and the crowd shouted 'Drive him out!' Halpin and Clyne seized [James Weldon] and were about to pull him out of the shop and beat him when the police interfered, and [Weldon] was able to escape by the back door ... The crowd then headed by Halpin and Clyne, and containing most, if not all, of the defendants, went to Father Tuite at the Parochial House, and

14

saw him there. They then came back to the Market Square and held an indignant meeting there.

Fr Tuite did not support the mob's demands to sack James Weldon.

Postman Tom Lenihan, one of the Weldon family's few supporters, told in sworn evidence later how Clyne asked the priest, 'Are you going to allow Master Weldon to teach school in Ballinvalley?' Patrick Corcoran challenged further. 'If you do, Fr Tuite, we won't.' In quoting the parish priest's answer, Lenihan's concluding evidence evoked an older trial by mob rule. Fr Tuite answered, 'Very well, do as you like'. A village Pilate washing his hands?

Later that evening, Patrick Corcoran told Tom Lenihan to keep his children from Ballinvalley school or get his cattle out of Corcoran's field. By this time, James Weldon was back in his home in Ballinvalley, but a crowd gathered at the Market Square in Delvin and lit a tar barrel. There was cheering and jostling as people announced their intent before casting a copy of *The Valley of the Squinting Windows* into the flames. To this day, families claim that more than one copy was burned, but that theirs was the first. Many years later, Nellie Weldon, Brinsley's sister, told of the affair and how some people of a quiet disposition in Delvin were threatened by the ring-leaders of the protest into boycotting her father's school. When asked if the characters in the book were based on real people, Nellie answered, 'If the cap didn't fit them, they needn't wear it'.

IN 1918, BALLINVALLEY (Male) National School, had an average of 30 enrolled students. On 29 May, the morning after the burning of his son's book, James Weldon arrived at his place of employment. He found seven pupils there, along with the assistant teacher. Three armed members of the Royal Irish Constabulary stood at the gateway. About 70 people marched up, representatives from the majority of the households in the village, and halted at the school. According to reports, some had been intimidated, and were almost forced from their homes. The *Westmeath Examiner* stated that Cloughan Volunteer Clubmen (members of the Irish Volunteer movement) were in the crowd. It told how a deputation entered the school and demanded the immediate resignation of James Weldon. They instructed him to vacate the school building. Weldon refused. His manager, Fr Tuite not being present, Weldon requested proof of the parish priest's support for the demand. Reports suggest that Joseph Clyne issued the instructions, and that Halpin, Corcoran and a man named Cully supported him. They pointed out that John Bray, who was to feature later, was not present.

Clyne was a tall, hefty, formidable man weighing over 16 stone. On RIC Sergeant Rody's insistence, the group sent for Fr Tuite. He arrived in an agitated state. He warned James Weldon that if the children did not return to the school, he would have to be dismissed. Weldon reminded the priest of the first Maynooth Resolution of 1894 adopted by the bishops of Ireland. It stipulated that three months' notice of dismissal could not be served on a teacher by a Catholic clerical manager without the bishop's consent. Furthermore, the teacher had the right to a hearing. Dismissing this, Fr Tuite issued the three months' notice to Weldon. Asking the people to disperse, he then ordered the assistant and pupils out of the school and locked the door. Reports suggest that, from the time of the visit of the crowd to the school on Wednesday morning, Mr Weldon was under police protection.

Fr Tuite contacted his bishop, Dr Gaughran, who forbade Weldon's dismissal. There was a Corpus Christi procession in Delvin on Thursday 30 May. At this annual ceremony, it was usual for the principal teacher of Ballinvalley to take charge of male pupils. Stewarding and other positions of authority were often handed down from one generation to the next and office-holders were proud of their roles. James Weldon was snubbed in the 1918 procession when two of his adversaries, Patrick Kearney, grocer, and Patrick Corcoran, farmer, got the task of looking after the Ballinvalley schoolboys. Some reports claim that an assistant teacher was asked to do the job but was unwilling to replace her principal. She offered an excuse and left Delvin for the day. When she returned that night, her pony-trap had been vandalised.

On Sunday 2 June, the protesters were dumbfounded. Announcing that Ballinvalley School would re-open the next morning, Fr Tuite stated from the pulpit, 'Wrong steps have been taken which we must redress'. Throughout Sunday, the ring-leaders encouraged, cajoled or intimidated parents into keeping their children away from Ballinvalley. They successfully arranged transport to other schools. Only 10 boys turned up for school on Monday. Most of these were from homes of the local workhouse staff. A few more returned during the week. On 4 June, James Weldon complained formally to the police. The *Westmeath Examiner* claimed that within a fortnight 30 boys were back, but subsequent averages recorded indicate that if this was so, they did not remain in attendance.

There was concern among the Cloghan Clubmen. Brinsley MacNamara was a popular member who often addressed their meetings. Michael Fox, Club leader, expelled those who were involved actively in the harassment of the schoolmaster. He issued a statement at a county Volunteer meeting in Mullingar, threatening action against any member who persisted with such conduct.

Delvin's small community was buzzing with rumour. Pickets occupied roads converging on the school. Some people alleged that the local RIC sergeant, Patrick Rody, had been bribed. More threatened to kidnap and expel Brinsley MacNamara. Those who felt libelled by *The Valley of the Squinting Windows* sought legal advice. In search of a solution, the local curate, Fr Cogan, approached parishioners. Either James Weldon had had a hand in writing the book or in passing on some of its content to his son, some protested. Others were venting their bitterness on James only because Brinsley, their real target, was not around. Most of them wanted Cogan to write to Mr E.A. Shaw, a Mullingar solicitor, instructing him to take an action against James Weldon and his author-son for criminal libel. They intended dropping this course of action if Weldon disavowed the book. (According to one source, he had already agreed to do this, in writing.) As a result of a later conversation between Cogan and Weldon, the schoolmaster wrote to Fr Tuite. He denied connection with the authorship or publication of the book and he apologised for any slight caused. Fr Cogan circulated this letter. He also read it from the altar at Mass on Sunday 7 July. Adding that the dispute was settled, he advised parents to send their children back to the school. For a day or two, some did. Then the initiative lost momentum and the Delvin people resumed the boycott.

The Weldon family bore severe humiliations. Most of the shops in the village refused to serve them. Tierneys did, and this resulted in many of their other regular customers taking their business elsewhere. While apologetic, Tierneys then ceased trading with Weldons. Remaining loyal to the distressed family, Tom Lenihan devised a scheme to supply them with foodstuffs. He and his family purchased more than they required for themselves; they spread their transactions over a number of shops so that nobody would notice this. After dark, some of the Weldon children would come across the fields to Lenihan's house in Ellenstown, outside Delvin, and collect the goods. The ruse was discovered and, in retribution, the Fitzsimons family joined the Corcorans in refusing grazing permission to Tom Lenihan.

Brinsley MacNamara considered emigration to England but decided instead to seek refuge at the home of his future wife in Quin, Co. Clare. Back at home, Fr Tuite, incensed by Brinsley's book itself and by its repercussions in his parish, turned against the Weldons. The storm blew strongly. Regular meetings about the affair took place on Tuesdays and Thursdays with a formal meeting every Sunday, under the chairmanship of the parish priest.

Benedict Kiely recalled hearing that people in Collinstown, five miles west of Delvin, used to cycle to Delvin on Sundays during the years after the book-burning, viewing places and people that the book was said to describe. There was even the chance of observing a fight or squabble between supporters and enemies of the Weldons. Local lore supports the sightseeing suggestion but not the fighting. Delvin was being held up to ridicule as more and more people heard about the boycott and other antics in the Garradrimna of Westmeath. Maunsel and Company, the Dublin publishing house, had printed 1,000 copies of *The Valley of the Squinting Windows*. When they heard about the furore in Delvin, they withdrew the title and made no further effort to publicise it.

The boycott of James Weldon's school continued and traders still refused to supply life's necessities to the family. James attempted to hire a motor car to attend his mother's funeral. Nobody obliged. Similar treatment continued throughout 1919. Towards the end of that year, Fr Cogan tried to have him removed. On 17 October, Cogan visited the school and James Weldon abused him in front of the pupils. He accused the priest of taking boys from the school to serve at High Masses in order to keep down the average. Fr Cogan alleged that Mr Weldon added:

> You are supporting the game and you are the constant companion of the crowd of ruffians and would-be murderers, Clyne, Halpin and Corcoran. You know they are murderers because they made a murderous attack on me and you spend all your time talking to them and you pass by the teachers of the parish without speaking to them, those that did the work in the past. I won't let it go any further. I will report you within a week to the Most Reverend Dr Gaughran.

After informing his parish priest of the incident, Cogan sought counsel from Mullingar solicitor J.J. Macken. Macken advised him to report the matter formally to Fr Tuite and to state that Weldon, 'in using such language without either justification or provocation, rendered himself liable to instant dismissal and that [Fr Tuite] as manager could forthwith exercise that right'. Cogan wrote. Alluding to Weldon's threat to write to the bishop, he stated, 'I am writing to you so that through you, His Lordship may be made fully cognisant of the facts'.

Fr Tuite was careful too. On 20 October he wrote to the Secretaries of the Education Board about Weldon's alleged outburst. They replied, seeking further particulars, including a statement from Cogan. Tuite then received a letter from James Weldon. Irreverently, perhaps, he had written on black-bordered mourning notepaper:

3 November 1919

On full reflection I beg leave to apologise to Father Cogan and am sorry that many annoyances caused me to lose my temper. I have heard you have reported me to the Commissioners [i.e. Education Board] and hope you will now be so good as to withdraw same.

Meanwhile Macken, the Mullingar solicitor, forwarded a copy of Cogan's complaint to the Commissioners. He also asked Tuite to send a further copy to Weldon and return to him any statements the teacher wished to make on the matter.

On 1 December 1919 James Weldon wrote a letter to Fr Tuite stating the reasons for his accusation. Only boys from his school, he pleaded, were taken to serve Mass. Those attending other parish schools because of the boycott were not taken. In Fr Cogan's presence, he claimed, he asked pupils about this and they all said that 'some of the priests' asked them. Weldon went on:

He then asked me did I believe that this was done with design, and I replied that in consequence of all I could see of his actions I could come to no other conclusion. I pointed out to him that from the day I was attacked by the mob led by Clyne, Corcoran and Halpin, who did their best to murder me and would have succeeded but for Constabulary being at hand to prevent it, he was constantly in the company of some of the men who took an active part against me, and that as far as I was aware a word of rebuke he never uttered with reference to their conduct or anything they did afterwards in trying to ruin the school.

Weldon told of how he had saluted Fr Cogan in the village and how his courtesy was not acknowledged; also, how the priest ordered boys from his school to attend coursing matches, thus compounding his low attendance problem. 'His manner towards me has always been dictatorial and overbearing, frequently insulting, and a word of sympathy

20

he never expressed towards me during the terrible ordeal I have been subjected to for the past year and a half,' he wrote.

In a covering note to the Education Board, Tuite requested an immediate investigation to 'dissipate the unworthy aspersions cast on Fr Cogan by the (perhaps disturbed) imagination of Mr Weldon'.

This further pressure brought action from the Board. On 7 January 1920 they sent Mr D.J. McEnery, District Inspector, to report on the boycott in general and on the incident involving Fr Cogan – formidable tasks. McEnery took statements from Fr Cogan, Mr Weldon, Fr Tuite and at least seven parents of children who had left Ballinvalley School and were studying elsewhere.

Much of the collected material covered old ground. Fr Cogan reiterated his case, adding that he helped increase averages by asking parents to return their children to Ballinvalley. While some complied initially, they took their children away again after a short period, he claimed.

Patrick and Lucia Kearney had sent their children to a friend in Killucan so that they could attend school there. They said that, even before the boycott, they were not making satisfactory progress in Ballinvalley. Fr Cogan asked them to return the children to Ballinvalley. They did, but were forced to remove them again because of the bad language they were picking up.

John and Anna Bray had sent a child to Collinstown school. They claimed that they had no quarrel with James Weldon in his treatment of their son, although they did not like him as a teacher. He failed to exercise proper control in class.

Jane and Michael Daly alleged that Mr Weldon called one of their three boys a tramp and wrongly punished another for tearing a book.

Mary Cully was outspoken and may have been the most truthful. She had two nephews attending Ballinvalley up to the boycott. 'As a result of the way I was referred to in the Book, I withdrew the boys,' she wrote. Mary Cully worked in Delvin Post Office, the same as Garradrimna's

21

'old bespectacled postmistress, already blinded partially, and bent from constant, anxious scrutiny, poring exultantly over the ... letter in her hand [which she then steamed open]'.

While it appears that Fr Cogan influenced parents and guardians to strengthen his own statement, one pupil, Patrick Tierney, stated that Fr Cogan granted him and a boy named Perrick a free day to go to a coursing match (hare chasing by greyhounds). They did not avail of the offer, choosing to attend school instead. In his own statement, Cogan admitted giving a delicate boy permission to take a day off school and go to the coursing match. As to James Weldon's allegation of partisanship, the priest claimed that he had the same sort of relationship with Clyne, Halpin and Corcoran, as he had with all his parishioners. He said that he had arrived in the parish on 9 May 1918, just before the book-burning incident. He described the MacNamara novel as 'scurrilous and libellous' and said that Fr Tuite was annoyed by it and by what it was doing to Ballinvalley School. He claimed to have done what he could to settle the dispute and, concerning the boycott, he wrote: 'Instead of assisting to keep down the average, I did more than a man's part to keep it up.'

James Weldon agreed in the main with Fr Cogan's statement. He recounted the events of 28 May 1918 and afterwards. Putting his attackers in charge of the procession was a great insult, he protested. So too was a more recent action of Fr Cogan's, when he gave a young man the task of teaching new altar boys how to serve Mass. Traditionally, this was the schoolmaster's function.

Fr Tuite, in his statement, wrote that the publication of *The Valley of the Squinting Windows* 'caused madness in the district'. He described Fr Cogan as 'most zealous and anxious for the welfare of the schools ... it was an extraordinary thing on the part of Mr Weldon to attack Fr Cogan in the school'. Tuite expressed a wish for a change of teacher and added, 'owing to the hostile attitude of the people towards the master, the attendance will never improve in his time'.

Elaborating on this later, Fr Tuite contended that Weldon's most hostile opponents would wish his departure to be attended by the least possible injury to the interests of himself and his family, but 'on the principle that the teacher is for the school, not the school for the teacher, if one or other is to be sacrificed, surely it is not the school?' In April 1920 the Board of Education severely reprimanded James Weldon for his behaviour towards Fr Cogan. They warned him that any similar misconduct would be visited with a serious penalty.

Two months later, on 23 June, in Clooney church, Quin, Co. Clare, Brinsley MacNamara (John Weldon), with an address at 17 Hume Street, Dublin, married local girl Helena (Lena) Degidon, whom he had met when she was teaching in Ballinvalley girls' school. So the daughter of Patrick Degidon and his late wife, Annie (Forde) of Rylane, became part of a family that was moving towards the climax of five years of strife. Lena had left Delvin in 1913 to take a teaching appointment in Corkscrew Hill, Co. Clare, then accepting another in her home town of Quin. She came to war-torn Dublin where a son, Oliver, was born on 16 May 1921. Later, she and her child returned to Quin, having decided to settle into peaceful village life for good.

During the passage of time, the Education Board Commissioners had more than the clerical complaint to worry about. The average attendance at Ballinvalley boys' school for 1919 was 17.7. This compared with an average of 36 in 1917 and 30 in 1918. A slight improvement during 1920 brought the figure up to 20, but it was back down to 17.7 in 1921. By 1922 it had fallen to 13.4. The National Education Office took action. They proposed the amalgamation of male and female schools (the latter having 47 on the roll).

The Board despatched a school inspector, J.A. McMahon, to investigate and report on the proposed amalgamation. He advised against it. He outlined the history of the case and articulated reasons why the locals viewed *The Valley of the Squinting Windows* as a libel on the village and locality. Stressing the decline in averages, he warned that if amalgamation took place, parents would not send their girls to school either. Consequently the staff and pupils of that school would suffer too. McMahon also pointed out that a case was due before the law courts and, given the strained relations this obviously caused between James Weldon and the locals, there was little chance of settlement until it was over. He felt that a decision on the amalgamation should be postponed until then.

Conscious of the distress his book was visiting on his father, Brinsley MacNamara wrote to Professor Michael Hayes, Minister for Education, on 2 August 1922. Under Department regulations, the drop in averages would bring about a decrease in salary and subsequent pension, so Brinsley recalled the 'circumstances of [his father's] position for the past four years ... which [were] now ... about to result in his immediate and complete victimisation'. He mentioned his father's long and faithful service during 40 years teaching in two Delvin parish schools. Regarding the 'pro-book and anti-book parties' and their actions, MacNamara gave credit for restoring law and order to the main body of the Volunteers and not to the RIC whom, he claimed, were won over by the mob. It was the continuing boycott, com-bined with the dwindling population in what had once been a large ranching district, that had brought the school average below the minimum needed to maintain his father's salary in his particular grade, he claimed. The trauma had also affected James Weldon's health, making his position more difficult still. Also, MacNamara pointed out, his father was within a year or two of retirement and, unless special allowances were made, his pension prospects were unfavourable. His appeal for consideration was disregarded and, with effect from 1 January 1923, James Weldon's salary dropped from £338 to £255.

A few weeks later, on 12 February, MacNamara again wrote to the Department. This time he pointed out that his father's salary had been reduced and that the continuing boycott was tantamount to forcing his resignation. He asked what was intended concerning Mr Weldon's pension, and the full extent of the likely loss, explaining that he needed the information for instructing a solicitor in an action against the conspirators.

On 10 April 1923 James Weldon issued a writ of summons against Fr Tuite and others for 'damages instanced by reason of the conspiracy of the defendants, their agents and servants to injure the plaintiff in his occupation as schoolteacher and being a malicious combination to boycott the school'. He also alleged that the defendants conspired to deprive him of his salary and so curtail his pension.

The stage was set for a legal show-down, where schoolmaster would take on his clerical manager and named neighbours in 'The Case of the Squinting Windows'.

BRINSLEY MACNAMARA DETESTED lies. Even his enemies, who regarded him as caustic or sneering attested to his integrity. Yet on 21 January 1923 he wrote a letter to Fr Tuite that was at best naive and foolish:

Ballinvalley,
Delvin,
21 January 1923

Sir,

I have been deputed by the Chief Executive Officer of National Education to interview you in connection with the present condition of Ballinvalley Boys' School and to discuss the matter so that certain arrangements may be made. The Chief Executive Officer of National Education believes you to be the Manager of Ballinvalley School. Your failure to grant me this interview has, however, confirmed me in the well-grounded suspicion that not you but certain persons, to whose illegal actions you have lent your sanctions and complicity, constitute the managing body of Ballinvalley School.

I am still open to be otherwise convinced upon this and notwithstanding the fact that because of your abominable treatment of my people here, it is indeed very distasteful to me to discuss with you any matter whatsoever. I am prepared to meet you at any hour you may name up to 2 p.m. tomorrow, Monday. Failing this, other and most drastic action will be taken so that you may be fully recovered to a sense of your grave responsibilities in the matter.

Yours etc.

Brinsley MacNamara

Fr Tuite despatched the letter to the Board of Education who, after considerable delay (29 November – a few days before the trial) wrote to MacNamara asking for an explanation, since he had no licence to take such action. No other correspondence on the subject is available, but MacNamara's letter seems like an ill-advised and desperate effort to forestall legal proceedings.

On 10 April 1923, a Writ of Summons was issued 'for damages instanced by the Plaintiff by reason of the conspiracy of the Defendants, their Agents and Servants to injure the Plaintiff in his occupation as School Teacher and being a malicious combination to boycott the Plaintiff's school'. The trial was set for 16 November 1923. In the event, it did not open until 5 December of that year.

The *Midland Reporter* of 6 December gave the court case four headlines: 'Delvin Schoolmaster's £4000 Claim'; 'Conspiracy Alleged against Parish Priest and Seven Others'; 'An Unusual Case from Co. Westmeath'; 'Story of Indignation Meeting and Burning of Son's Book'. Some Delvin people took the train to Dublin from Athboy station for the trial.

They discussed the latest news, including a rumour that one defendant had signed over his property to his wife so that, if convicted, he could plead inability to pay a fine. Tom Lenihan and one of the Duffys travelled the day before. They wanted to leave a broken watch into Jameson's of Lower Sackville Street for repairs. As the assistant was writing down the Delvin address he expressed his disapproval of the disgraceful book Brinsley MacNamara had written about the place. Next morning Lenihan noticed the same man on the jury panel. He informed Weldon's counsel of the incident. Their objection to his serving on the jury was sustained. In the light of the eventual outcome, this may have been significant.

Many years later, Brinsley's sister, Nellie Weldon, recalled her mother saying the case should never have been brought to court because a priest was involved. She was a sensible woman, if the story told to Benedict Kiely by the writer Philip Rooney was true.

26

Heading for Navan races, Philip and a clergyman friend visited Crinnion's Hotel. The clergyman took a few drinks too many and talked loudly about various matters, ecclesiastical and otherwise. Philip was very gentlemanly; he got a little bit worried for the cleric's sake and said, 'Father, I think we'll move into the residents' lounge because, you know, if some of those remarks got back to the bishop!'

The priest answered, 'Philip, no bishop can touch me. I'm the man [who] drilled the witnesses in the Weldon case.'

The case opened on 5 December 1923 before Lord Justice O'Connor and a special jury. At the time of the case, it was common practice for newspapers to report proceedings verbatim. The *Westmeath Examiner*, the *Midland Reporter* and *The Irish Times* all carried near identical coverage. The reportage opened with a list of the defendants in the case. Along with Fr Tuite, these were Michael Cully (farmer); Patrick Halpin (butcher); Joseph Clyne (butcher); Patrick Corcoran (farmer); Thomas Fitzsimons, senior (retired publican); Patrick Kearney (grocer) and John Bray (farmer).

They were charged with conspiring to injure the plaintiff in his occupation of schoolteacher by means of a malicious combination to boycott his school, and with loss and damage by intimidation and otherwise; these charges were denied by the defendants. James Weldon was represented by Sergeant Hanna, Mr Jellett, KC and Mr Martin Maguire (instructed by Messrs Malley and Charles); Fr Tuite by Mr Lardner, KC, and Mr Geoghegan (instructed by J.J. Macken); Halpin and Corcoran by Mr Lynch, KC, Mr Denning and Mr Walsh (instructed by Messrs N.J. Downes and Co.); and Clyne, Kearney, Cully and Bray by Mr Meredith, KC, Mr Wood, KC, and Mr Hamilton (instructed by E.A. Shaw). The case was heard before Lord Justice O'Connor and a special jury.

What follows is a digest of the trial reports from 5-8 December:

Sergeant Hanna opened by stating that the plaintiff was seeking £4000 in damages, and went on to give an account of the events of 28 and 29 May ... Weldon had apparently been threatened with his son's arrest or kidnap if he failed to withdraw from the school. After three weeks he was forced to sign an agreement that he would apologise [this is the only mention of written intent to apologise]. At this the judge interjected: 'Apologise for what, Sergeant; for having a son?' to which Hanna replied, 'I suppose that would be it, my lord'. A promise to withdraw the boycott at this point was not fulfilled, however, and on 22 June Weldon wrote to Fr Tuite saying that he had nothing to do with the publication of the book and disavowing anything distasteful or undesirable in it. This, Hanna said, was done solely to relieve his mind of the terrible strain and in spite of his unwillingness to cringe to the murderous mob which had so savagely attacked him. As regards the Fr Cogan incident, Weldon claimed that he had defended himself and as a result was reported for discourtesy.

Weldon, called to give evidence, asserted that he was generally believed in Delvin to be the author of the book. In response to the judge's comment, 'I suppose you could not write a book like that to save your life,' he said, 'I never wrote a letter to the newspaper even in my life'. Cross-examined by Lynch, he went on to say that he had known nothing of his son's writing the book, the first intimation he got of its publication being from Fr Tuite in mid-May 1918.

Lynch, having established that Weldon had read the American edition of *The Valley*, asked, 'Does the preface state the characters are taken from real life?' Weldon replied, 'He stated that he wrote from what he saw'. Lynch defended the relevance of further queries on the grounds that he would prove certain people were mentioned in the book. This exchange followed:

Lynch: Can you point to a single redeeming character in the book except the old schoolmaster?

28

Weldon: I am not a literary critic and I would not be able to answer you that.

Lynch: Isn't it a fact that the priests, farmers, traders, and schoolteachers, except the old schoolmaster, were all held up to ridicule and contempt in the book?

Weldon: I don't think so.

Lynch: You would not think it right to describe a clergyman as 'the flirtatious boy of the district?'

Weldon: I did not describe him in any such terms.

[This final answer suggests confusion and distortion, with Weldon being asked to explain and defend someone else's work.]

Tom Lenihan testified to seeing Weldon being dragged out of North's shop by Halpin, assisted by Clyne. He gave an account of verbal exchanges between Clyne and Tuite at the Parochial House.

DAY TWO

Patrick Rody, an ex-RIC sergeant, estimated that between 40 and 60 people had turned up at the school on 29 May. He intervened, ordering them to send for Fr Tuite. In reply to the judge, Rody described the crowd as peaceful but agreed that 40 or 60 going into a shop to bring a man out was very curious. In cross-examination, Rody said that he had interviewed Weldon on the night of 28 May and saw no mark of an assault on him.

John O'Rourke, a police constable, testified to seeing an angry crowd of about 35 or 40, including all the defendants except Bray and Fr Tuite, outside Clyne's pub; some of them were under the influence of drink. On reaching North's they rushed in, on some signal from Cully. The police were just behind and O'Rourke saw Clyne and Halpin in grips with Weldon, dragging him along while the crowd shouted, 'Pull him out, pull him out'. O'Rourke got between Clyne and Halpin, shoved Clyne out and got Weldon back into the house. He described the crowd as very threatening; they waited for about five minutes shouting to get back in, till he

29

put his hand on the holster of his revolver and said, 'If you don't get back you will have to take the consequences'. On their return from the Parochial House, there was hooting and booing as they passed North's house. He estimated the crowd at the school the following morning at about 60.

Thomas Heslip, another policeman, claimed that Clyne responded to Rody's remonstrations by saying, 'Weldon should be strung up like a fox for the hounds', though Rody, who was recalled later, did not remember this comment. This conveyed to Heslip the meaning that Weldon should be lynched. Lynch provoked laughter by retorting, 'Don't bring the Lynches into it at this stage'. Heslip also attested to having on several occasions protected Weldon's house and escorted him in the village, precautions that were necessary for the greater part of that summer. Thomas Weldon corroborated this account of the family's treatment, giving evidence of having been refused goods in shops until the police came with him. He also testified that his brother had never discussed the book with him, nor had he ever heard of it until it was published.

Patrick Casey, District Councillor at the time, claimed to have been at the head of the crowd going to the school, whose principal object was, he said, peace. He alone of all the defendants gave evidence that it had been arranged to picket the roads to the school. The general opinion was that Weldon had given his son the information written in the book, and people would have been satisfied if he had disavowed it. Casey, who acknowledged the existence of a family quarrel with James Weldon, answered the judge's comments on condemning a man unheard with, 'Well, considering I was described in the book myself.' Asked if he thought his actions were fair, he replied, 'As we knew it at the time, it was fair enough'. He had withdrawn from the others, he said, because they did not support him enough, at which the judge observed, 'I wonder is there much worse said about the people of Delvin in the book than you have said now.'

At the close of the case for the plaintiff, Meredith was granted a direction in favour of John Bray, with costs to be considered afterwards. Similar requests on behalf of Fr Tuite, Halpin and Corcoran were refused. Addressing the jury for Halpin and Corcoran, Lynch commented that the author at least must be delighted with the proceedings, which repaid him for his financial and other assistance to the plaintiff with 'an advertisement that has secured for him, probably for all time, a position that will take him from the obscurity from which he might not otherwise have emerged'. Pointing out that parents were entitled to choose any school they liked for their children, Lynch said there was no evidence of picketing or boycotting. He cast doubt on the assertion that the Weldon family had known nothing of the book until it was published, and defended the indignant reaction of people lampooned and caricatured in it and their right to question Weldon on his part in it. The events of 29 May were of a most harmless kind, while those of 28 [were] outbursts of feeling on the part of the people in Delvin. The plaintiff, he said, had not proved anything that was necessary to prove in order to succeed in his action.

Meredith, who followed, attributed the falling off in school attendance to war conditions, the closing of the workhouse and barracks in the district, a quarrel between Weldon and Fr Cogan, Weldon's illness and his vindictive treatment of pupils.

Fr Tuite gave evidence that a crowd of about 20 came to his door on 28 May, impassioned to get rid of Weldon. Tuite pointed out that it was not easy to get rid of a teacher, to which one replied: 'We will hunt him.' Weldon promised the priest to write a statement saying that he had nothing to do with the authorship of the book. In response to the judge's question, 'Did you think it was unjust to visit the sins of the son upon the father?' Tuite said, 'There is something unjust about it'.

31

Fr Cogan, who on 9 May had been appointed to the parish with the school specifically put under his charge, stated that shortly before 28 May he got to know there was trouble in the parish. Cogan attested to the common belief that Weldon was the author of the book but denied the existence of a boycott, admitting only to public indignation, which he did his best to put down. He refuted the suggestion that he had asked Weldon to sign a statement, saying that his son would be arrested otherwise. He had, he said, arranged an agreement between the teacher and the villagers whereby Weldon would write a letter to Fr Tuite disavowing all connection with the publication and authorship of the book and the villagers would withdraw legal proceedings against him and his son. When the letter arrived, Cogan was instructed by the defendants and others to write to Mr Shaw, solicitor, of Mullingar, withdrawing the action of criminal libel against James and John Weldon.

The next witness was Joseph Clyne, who stated that the book had given great offence; the judge observed that the truth sometimes gave offence. Clyne described leaving the church on 28 May and joining a crowd on the way to Fr Tuite's. On passing North's, someone had suggested bringing Weldon out with them to give an explanation. Clyne went over to the door and said to Weldon, sitting inside, 'There is a deputation going down to Fr Tuite over this book which we believe you and your son wrote ...' He was interrupted when Weldon, rising and raising his stick, tried to assault him. Clyne denied catching Weldon by the throat and claimed that he would have been seriously assaulted had not Halpin caught the stick. He also denied speaking at the Parochial House and addressing the Market Square meeting, asking people to go to the school the next morning. He had not called for recruits for picketing; nor, to his knowledge, had anyone else. As regards the alleged statement that Weldon should be strung up like a fox for the hounds, he said that he never used his tongue in such a way. In the scene at the school on 29 May, he had neither informed

Weldon that he had been sent by Tuite nor driven out the children and assistant teacher. He described following Tuite into the school and hearing Weldon say: 'This is a nice state of affairs the Brannigans and the Shannons have brought on.' Replying to the judge he said that these were names given in the book. He had heard no mention of dismissal or notice at the school, and denied all allegations of subsequent conspiracy, intimidation and obstruction. On Clyne's putting the number at the school at about 35 or 40, the judge said: 'If you are ever sending a deputation to any of the Ministers in Merrion Street, it should be more limited in number,' causing laughter in the court.

Halpin, following, gave a similar account of the events of 28 May; he denied trying to drag Weldon into the street and confirmed Clyne's account of Weldon's attempted assault and his own intervention. He too asserted his innocence on all picketing charges. Cully, Corcoran and Kearney did likewise, with Cully adding that he thought the whole thing was over on 7 July 1918 [when Fr Tuite announced as much at Mass in Delvin]. Thomas Fitzsimons, the remaining defendant, was ill and unable to attend the trial.

Mrs Merriman then testified that no one had ever asked her to withdraw her children from the school, and that when, at Fr Cogan's request, she had brought them back, Weldon said: 'You brought them back because you had to. You can bring them back [again now] to your drunken husband.'

Witnesses then gave evidence that Weldon had beaten pupils [and] called them 'tramps'.

This closed the case for the defendants.

Weldon was then recalled and gave the average attendances at the school between January 1916 and December 1922. His salary had [been] diminished by £161 and his loss on the capitation grant would be £14. The loss in pension, if the 10% reduction were taken into consideration, would be £72 a year. Replying to Hanna, Weldon contradicted Fr Cogan, saying that the document he signed, which apologised for offence given by the book, had been dictated by the curate, who told him that his son would be arrested if

33

he failed to sign. Cogan also assured him that he would see to it that the children were sent back to the school. There was, said Weldon, no question whatever of legal proceedings being brought against him or his son. He also denied the allegations of beatings. On Weldon's saying that publication of the book had been stopped by letter, the judge enquired whether this remained the case. Lynch replied that the ban was lifted after these proceedings.

Counsel for the defendants addressed the jury, contending that there was no evidence of conspiracy. The judge made a distinction between Tuite and the other defendants, saying that he thought the priest stood differently from the rest and did not think that he was in the movement against the teacher.

DAY FOUR

Meredith delivered a summing-up to the jury on behalf of Clyne, Kearney and Cully, followed by Jellett on behalf of Weldon. Meredith described the evidence as proving only that there had been an 'epidemic of indignation' in Delvin against James Weldon and his son. The events of 28 May were, he said, spontaneous; the people involved were respectable and not of the criminal type. If the alleged assault was taken out of the case, no illegal action was suggested against them. On 29 May, the crowd went to get a disclaimer from Weldon that this book had anything to do with Delvin, wanting the message to go to the people of Ireland that there was no gross immorality going on in the town of Delvin, and that the people there were not like the characters portrayed in the book. Weldon was to disavow the authorship as well as the suggestions in the book; this, said Meredith, he would have done at once if he had the sense of a tom-tit, and that would have been the end of it. Weldon, however, was an obstinate man and had taken up a fighting attitude at once. He ended by reiterating the alleged causes for the drop in attendance – war conditions, etc.

34

Jellett, closing for Weldon, referred to his long and creditable career as a teacher and his previously cordial relations with the Delvin villagers. The people who joined the crowd on 28 and 29 May were all out for the same purpose, as clear from the statement reported by Fr Tuite: 'We will hunt him.' The theory advanced by the defendants was, said Jellett, blown to pieces by the priest's testimony that the dispute was going on to the present moment. He criticised Tuite, both in his capacity as parish priest and as school manager, for not taking a clear stand against the actions of the defendants. The total loss to James Weldon in the figures put down was about £1,740, but the jury was urged not to confine damages to that amount, given the plaintiff's present position as outcast in the village. If this sort of thing was allowed to go on, ended Jellett, there would be no real social life in Ireland.

Justice O'Connor then addressed the jury, reminding them that the main question was whether there had been a conspiracy to boycott. If there was a conspiracy to secure Weldon's dismissal, said the judge, then the plaintiff had suffered no loss on that behalf as he had never been dismissed. He went on to the question of John Weldon's [Brinsley MacNamara's] having given financial assistance to his father in this action. The judge defended the author's right to provide such support.

Some reference to the book was, he stated, essential, both from the plaintiff's and the defendants' points of view; the former had to suggest some motive for the defendants' conduct towards him, and the latter insisted that it gave great offence, with the result that they were up in arms against it. Extended references, however, were not relevant; without scrutinising the book and then the lives of every person mentioned in it, the jury could not know whether it was a good book or a bad one, true or false. [Here, as elsewhere in the trial, Justice O'Connor seems to accept that the villagers were indeed portrayed in the novel.]

He commented on the Irish propensity to be led and suggested that in this instance Casey might have been the agitator. The case rested on what the jurors believed the objective of the defendants to be in the events of 28 and 29 May: to prevent Weldon functioning in his school or to approach him as a peaceful deputation and ask if he was responsible for the book. He went on to deride the idea of 30 or 40 men being described as a deputation and to stress the importance of Casey's evidence. If they accepted his testimony that an agreement had been made at the open-air meeting to boycott the school, it was very difficult to avoid the conclusion that there had been a conspiracy. The attendance at the school had dropped from 43 to 13.7 and the defendants, if guilty, would be liable as long as the results of the conspiracy lasted. The judge expressed his sympathy for Fr Tuite, a very old man put in a position of extreme difficulty; there was, he said, no evidence against him. If the plaintiff was right, he concluded, he was entitled to substantial damages.

The jury, after an absence of 40 minutes, failed to agree. They were directed to find a verdict for Bray, entering costs, and were then discharged.

BRINSLEY MACNAMARA HAD prepared a brief and stood by to give evidence, but he was not called. The *Evening Herald* made the case its lead story for four days, contributing further details of the testimony. It reported James Weldon's description of Fr Tuite coming to the school, holding up his hand and saying, 'I dismiss you, you are no use to me any longer', at which the Judge remarked, 'When you say he held up his hand, was it in benediction or in surrender to a superior force?' He drew laughter from the crowded public gallery. There was also further elaboration of His Lordship's summing up:

> There ought to be a bit of give and take in these matters ... They had for such a long period of time been holding themselves up – and rather unsuccessfully – as a country unparalleled in sanctity and scholarship that he was afraid their national character was in some danger of degeneration, and he was afraid he himself and some other people as well, used to wish there never had been a saint or scholar in Ireland (*Laughter*). At any rate their national conceit had got some little knock in the last few

years and perhaps they would all be the better of it when they came to face the actual facts of life in this country.

The *Irish Independent* felt 'it was a pity, after so much expense had been incurred' that the jury failed to agree. It was said that this happened because of just one man holding out in favour of James Weldon. (Before 1967 a jury verdict had to be unanimous. With Philip Rooney's story in mind, was this dissenter the substitute juror, and were more than the witnesses in the case drilled?)

When John Bray came home with his £90 in costs, the boycott committee took the money off him to help offset expenses. This and details of transport organisation suggest that the boycott was tightly organised.

Literary Dublin registered pique, but there was no surge of protest on behalf of freedom of expression. However, a few defended a novelist's right to present things as he saw them, to base fiction upon fact. Realising that James Weldon and Brinsley MacNamara had suffered financially and were in no position to have the case reopened, a group organised an appeal for funds. Among these were W.B. Yeats, George W. Russell (A.E.), Oliver St John Gogarty, James Stephens and James G. Douglas.

Although some important names in literature signed, a few who might have been expected to support the appeal demurred. George Bernard Shaw was, as ever, practical:

> 10 Adelphi Terrace, with Bernard Shaw's compliments.
>
> I return these as they may be useful to you. The case does not seem to me to be one to make a public stand on. It is hard on Mr Weldon that his legal remedy has failed and it should have lain in the criminal, not in the civil courts. But I see no good in throwing good money after bad trying to get a jury to agree in a case of that nature.
>
> G.B.S.

Lord Justice O'Connor's address as reported in the press, together with his charges outlined by the Appeal Fund secretary suggest that an appeal might have succeeded. The attempt to raise funds, however, realised only a small sum, completely inadequate to contemplate reopening the case. James Weldon's health declined rapidly from this point on, but he remained obdurate.

Brinsley MacNamara did not relent either. On 16 January 1924 he called to the Board of Education and demanded the return of his father's roll-books that had been taken for the trial and not given back. He also sought Ministerial intervention against the continuing boycott, but was told that the Minister could not resolve the issue while low averages continued. MacNamara then asked if his father could be given a full pension by retiring immediately. Under the circumstances this would have seemed a sensible solution, but pension rules were statutory, so the proposal was rejected.

Another fact emerged just then. In a new summary of the case, Education Board memoranda contended that after the book-burning and initiation of the boycott, a decision was taken in Delvin, by whom it is not clear, that Maunsel's should suspend further publication. This suggests that James Weldon may have been forced not only to repudiate *The Valley of the Squinting Windows* but also to halt further production of the book. In any event, copies arrived in the country from the United States, where it was published by Brentano.

Minor harassment of the schoolteacher continued. The Board of Education accused him of absence without notice from his school when an inspector called to collect roll-books and other registers for the trial earlier. The Board played a game of convenience towards Brinsley's representations: they considered the case still to be *sub-judice* and therefore not open for comment.

The 81-year-old Fr Patrick Tuite died on 14 June 1924. During a ministry that began on 24 April 1892, he had completed church-building at Killulagh and cleared its debt. He had pointed and renovated Delvin church, and purchased a site for a new cemetery. However, it is for featuring in *The Valley of the Squinting Windows* case that he is remembered.

Reverend James Flynn succeeded him as parish priest. In his first sermon in Delvin he said: 'I stand before you in fear and trepidation.' On 20 February 1925 he wrote to the Board of Education, referring to the Weldon case, stating that James Weldon had tendered his resignation to Mr McMahon, inspector, and was about to submit it to him as school manager.

The priest expressed his conviction that, with a good man as teacher, Ballinvalley Boys' School would be 'one of the biggest in the country outside the towns'. This Irish bull accompanied further facts on averages: there were still only 20 or 21 on the roll and Delvin boys were travelling long distances to other schools. He assured the Board that he was 'not trying to work a job of any kind'.

On 27 February James Weldon resigned. Some time after that, he suffered a heart attack and was unconscious for four days. The Board pressed its opportunity to effect amalgamation. Fr Flynn was dogged. After arriving in Delvin he had announced from the altar that the children were illiterate leaving school. Ballinvalley was 'a flourishing school before Weldon' and would be again. The priest succeeded in resisting amalgamation and Thomas Healy of Edenderry National School was appointed to replace James Weldon. Within days of his taking over, the number of pupils on the roll jumped to 40. On 10 June, Fr Flynn proudly informed the Board that it had risen to 49. He sought and obtained a Junior Assistant Mistress.

By 12 October Fr Flynn was demanding a permanent assistant teacher. His claim that the daily attendance was then 58 or 59 is not borne out by official figures. Nevertheless, the rapid improvement must have been galling for James Weldon. From the teacher's residence he continued to occupy, he watched his old schoolhouse thrive. It is difficult to feel anything but pity for him.

On 27 January 1926 an assistant mistress was appointed to Ballinvalley Boys' School. The boycott was over, the Valley had won its way. In the spring of 1926, broken in health and spirit, James Weldon moved away from Delvin forever, to Valleymount, Avoca, Co. Wicklow.

39

POSTSCRIPT

In 1990 I published a book about the Delvin affair, *The Burning of Brinsley MacNamara* (Lilliput, Dublin). Benedict Kiely was kind enough to remark of it 'This, sure as God, is the book about the book'. While researching the work, it appeared that opinions in Delvin were still divided, mainly on family lines. But the good people were co-operative. I had been warned that some would be hostile towards me – far from it, they were civil and courteous. The folklore that had built up over the years was often, it transpired, based on gossip, not fact. Yet an offer made to host a launching of my book in Delvin was withdrawn. Certain sources alleged that the person who made the offer, not a native of Delvin, was briefed and advised to demur. Later still, a person who had given me considerable assistance when I was preparing the book, behaved in a truculent fashion because some of my views on Brinsley MacNamara disagreed with his. *The Valley of the Squinting Windows* can still raise hackles!

But at least my book was not burned. I think!

JAMES GRALTON – DEPORTEE

Conditions on small farms in County Leitrim were dismal in the 1920s. Impoverished householders joined their Donegal neighbours in the potato fields of Scotland to supplement incomes. Tenants in some of the uneconomic plots owed rents to absentee landlords whose kin had received large estates from King William for helping him beat James II. Michael Gralton, a Fenian, had a marshy holding at Effernagh, about six miles from Drumsna. He worked hard at home and helped to organise and run Kiltoghert Co-operative Creamery. Michael's wife, Alice gave birth to her second son on 17 April 1886. This boy, James, went to Kiltoghert national school and became friendly with his teacher, Master Duignan. He read more than most boys of his age, and took note of the misery on farms even smaller than his father's. Rearing a family of seven was difficult in those days and, like many before him, James tried to ease his parents' burden by leaving school as soon as he received Confirmation. He worked for a grocer in Carrick-on-Shannon, later for a publican-politician. After a short spell in a Dublin business house, he joined the British army. There is a record of his rebuking a chaplain in Fermoy, Co. Cork, who remonstrated with him for refusing a transfer to India. This may have been the first of a series of clashes with clergymen.

James deserted and went to Liverpool, then to a Welsh coal mine. Later on, he became a stoker on a steamer. In 1907, he came home for a short while before emigrating to the United States. In New York, he tried his hand at bar-tending, factory-work, cab-driving, and bread and ice delivery. At 22 years of age he was a committed socialist. He joined the Irish-American republican revolutionary movement, Clan na Gael, or the United Brotherhood. This oath-bound, secret organisation considered the Irish Republican Brotherhood (IRB) to be the true government of Ireland. Gralton soon left it to join the Communist Party. He raised money for the alleviation of poverty in New York and for sending home to help finance the Irish Republican Army (IRA).

Three weeks before the Truce of 11 July 1921, James Gralton returned to Effernagh. He occupied a disused building and, using his military knowledge, instructed the local battalion of the IRA in arms and in socialist thinking. When he began using his fellow guerillas to build a hall on his father's holding, the local clergy became worried. Forebodings of one Fr McGaver included predictions that Gralton would grow horns and that the horses used for carting materials to the project would die within one year. They did not, but the new Pearse and Connolly Hall opened to the public. Locals simply called it Gralton's Hall. It became the hub of social life in south Leitrim, but Gralton also organised post-primary education in Irish, music, woodwork, Irish dancing and English. His old schoolmaster's son, Tom Duignan, helped. The hall housed Republican Courts too. Now the clergy got really worried. In their view, control over any form of education should not be lost to a layman, particularly this one! Might James Gralton not be informing the young people about other things? Communism, for example! He might even be a Russian agent! It was time to speak out. They called Gralton an anti-Christ and his hall a den of iniquity.

A Treaty with Britain gave independence to 26 of Ireland's 32 counties and set men who had fought to achieve independence at each other's throats in a dreadful civil war. In Leitrim, farmers were complaining about grazing rights, the cost of living, over-holding of turf banks, and inadequate creamery payments. They organised cattle drives off large estates and formed a Direct Action Group to co-ordinate seizures of land. Gralton took the anti-Treaty side and the part of protesters of many shades. He drilled, arbitrated and presided over republican courts in his hall at Effernagh, Gowel, Co. Leitrim. In one incident, Gralton and a friend ignored threats of being shot by members of the National Army escorting a Drumsna curate. This happened outside a

farm that the Direct Action Group were about to have vacat-
in favour of someone they considered more deserving.
Gralton's party outflanked the army officer and cleric who
barred the entrance gate and expedited the transfer. Little
wonder the parish became known as 'The Gowel Soviet'.

In some of these direct action activities, up to 600 men
took part. This was a remarkable number, given the sparse
population in the Leitrim countryside so ravished by the
Famine and subsequent neglect from the establishment. At
that time too, there was no Labour votemob whatsoever in
Leitrim. In the election the following year four Cumann na
nGaedheal and three Republican candidates won seats.

Eventually the government issued a proclamation
denouncing commandeering, interference and trespass and
threatening severe penalties against perpetrators. Early in
May 1922, the army arrested James Gralton and took him to
Custume Barracks, Athlone. During his week's detention
there, supporters in south Leitrim staged demonstrations
and demanded his release. They greeted his return to Pearse
and Connolly Hall with fervour. There was a well-attended
dance in the hall on 24 May. The army surrounded the
building and called on the dancers to vacate it. They refused
at first, but when the army threatened to burn them out, they
slowly emerged. This gave James Gralton enough time to
escape from the hall. The soldiers took a number of his male
followers to Carrick-on-Shannon jail and held them there.
Their womenfolk arrived and protested vigorously until, a
fortnight later, the authorities released them. By that time,
however, the army had captured someone they wanted
more. James Gralton was in jail. Not for long, however. In a
country that fervently chronicles daring escapades and gallant escape bids, it is strange indeed to peruse assorted
accounts of James Gralton's life and times and note their lack
of detail on this important incident. None says how he
escaped.

On the run now, he heard about the Redemptorist missioners in Gowel denouncing the evils of foreign ideology,
especially Communism. They thumped the pulpit and

43

screamed about Gralton's Hall housing a Communist cell and being a danger to young people's morals and faith. James Gralton moved away from the area he hoped to free from assorted tyrannies. He narrowly escaped arrest in Drumsna but eventually reached Dublin, where he arranged his passage to New York.

AFTER THE CIVIL War, those who had opposed the Treaty found it difficult to obtain employment. This added to their grievances and created an environment in which socialist thinking thrived. In 1923, a Cumman na nGaedhal Minister for Agriculture, Patrick Hogan, introduced a new Land Act. 'The Hogan Act' provided for compulsory sale and purchase of certain estates and reduced rents fixed before 1911 by 35% and later rents by 30%. Potential beneficiaries who expected significant compulsory acquisition of big estates became disillusioned, however. In 1924, Peadar O'Donnell, editor of *An Phoblacht*, broke away from the IRA and founded the Republican Congress. It aimed at establishing a workers' republic. It did not last long, but O'Donnell, joined by Frank Ryan and George Gilmore, then formed Saor Eire, a socialist-republican group that aimed at overthrowing British imperialism and capitalism. They also sought public ownership of transport and control of land. Again, their land policy was attractive to south Leitrim. Marxist Revolutionary Workers' Groups appeared too. The climate for advancing socialism was improving.

James Gralton, meanwhile, was raising further small sums of money in America and sending it to poverty-stricken south Leitrim citizens. His hall back home was out of use but he sent cash for re-roofing it. Letters from him appeared in socialist publications. Along with a number of other Irishmen, he assisted in the formation of the powerful International Transport Workers' Union, initially based in New York. Among his associates were Michael Quill of Co. Kerry and Austin Hogan of Cork. They were members of the Communist Party of the United States.

James began to suffer from stomach trouble. Charles Gralton, who was running the farm in Leitrim, died in 1930. His parents were old, so James returned to help. Right away, he became embroiled in land agitation. Again the clergy began to berate him publicly, especially when he re-opened Gralton's Hall. He countered their claims and invited the Communist Party to set up a Revolutionary Workers' Group in Gowel.

There were two great public expressions of fervour in 1932. On 3 April, 15,000 Republicans marched from Sallins station to Wolfe Tone's grave in Bodenstown cemetery. Gralton led his Leitrim Revolutionary Workers in a contingent representing county cells. Jim Larkin Junior was at the head. A red banner bearing a hammer and sickle also carried the slogan, 'The Men of No Property'. For the four days between 22-26 June, the Eucharistic Congress celebrated the 1,500th anniversary of St Patrick's arrival in Ireland. There is no report that Gralton attended! The two events, occurring so close together, polarised feelings. Considering de Valera's Fianna Fáil a radical party that would release republican prisoners and attend to land injustices, James Gralton formed a branch in Drumsna and threw himself into assorted projects for the betterment of his supporters. After just a few months, party headquarters learned about his membership of Revolutionary Workers and prepared to expel him. A friend tipped him off and advised resignation. He complied. *The Communist Party in Ireland: An Outline History* by Sean Nolan (Dublin undated) remarked:

> The Revolutionary Workers' Group and the IRA Republicans demanded that the Free State CID should be disbanded. Typical of the De Valera Government's capability for compromising policies, most of the CID were transferred to other police duty ... Soon Fianna Fáil created the Broy Harriers, later to be known as the CID.

The *Irish Workers' Voice* pointed out that, in condoning all these actions against the militant working-class movement, the de Valera government was showing itself in its true colours – 'the agents of some of the blackest reactionary forces in the country'.

The *Irish Workers' Voice* of 18 February 1933 pointed out that the Gralton case was no isolated one and cited attacks on the Castlecomer miners and their trade union; 'murderous' campaigns by Cork priests against the unemployed; the hounding and persecution of members of the Revolutionary Workers' groups in Longford, Kilkenny, Waterford and in 'scores of other places throughout the country'. There were 'persistent pressures and hounding of printers to prevent the publication of the *Irish Workers' Voice* which was forced to go to a printer in Glasgow', the publication claimed.

James Gralton spoke against capitalism at an eviction protest, and clergy in other parishes besides Gowel joined in denouncing him. They accused him of being a Communist anti-Christ and Russian agent, running a den of vice in Effernagh. Peadar O'Donnell had warned Gralton not to take them on openly. He did, and was about to suffer.

The Hall Committee got worried. They approached their most outspoken priest and invited him to become their chairman. Fr O'Dowd refused but said he would take deeds of ownership and would nominate his own committee. The deputation need not have bothered asking James Gralton for his endorsement. He flatly refused. Seán Nolan's *Outline History* comments:

> Fr O'Dowd drew upon the action of the Northern Ireland Unionist regime which had, in the 1932 unemployment riots, used an old British Act of Parliament to deport back to Britain the veteran working-class writer Tom Mahon who had gone to Belfast to help the unemployed struggles. Fr O'Dowd demanded that 'All Communists' should be deported, and claimed there were fourteen of them in his parish. He also stated that 'Those attending the hall do so at their own risk', and warned the parish not to blame him for 'what might happen'. Those looking for relief work might not look to him to help them get it unless they quit attending the hall. And to rub it in thoroughly, he demanded that every one of the 'offenders' apologise to him for having flouted his authority. The neighbouring boys and girls of the place apparently chose to judge for themselves on the issue and continued to meet and dance in the hall.

Local lore, preserved in an excellent biography of Gralton by Desmond Guckian, tells one amusing anecdote of the time. A Gowel man named Scollan met an old woman in a neighbouring district. When he told her where he was from, she enquired about 'the terrible anti-christ, Gralton'. She wanted to know was it true that he once set fire to a lake. Scollan said it was. She then asked him how Gralton had put out the fire. 'Simple,' Scollan replied, 'he pissed on it.'

James Gralton persisted with spreading the fire of workers' unrest. He addressed a large meeting in Longford and the Bishop of Ardagh and Clonmacnoise joined in the condemnations. Lukewarm supporters became concerned and drifted away. By the end of 1932, the local IRA had turned against him. During a dance in the hall towards the end of November, enemies fired shots, holing the roof and smashing windows. Gralton shouted at the dancers to throw themselves on the floor. As soon as they did, the shooting stopped and the dance continued. The *Workers' Voice* was proud of that. About a week later, an attempt failed to blow up the hall by exploding a mine. On Christmas Eve 1932, Gralton's enemies threw petrol over the hall and set fire to it. The blaze destroyed the building.

An election was coming up and clergymen sat on Fianna Fáil electioneering platforms. The sitting Minister for Justice was the Longford-Westmeath Fianna Fáil barrister, James Geoghegan. One of his last acts in office was the signing of a deportation order in respect of James Gralton. The document described Gralton as an undesirable alien. It was served just after the funeral of James' father on 1 February 1935. Patrick Ruttledge (Mayo North) became Justice Minister in the new Fianna Fáil government on 8 February. James Gralton sought a meeting with him. He also looked for a trial. Neither was granted. Old supporters rallied round and formed a defence committee. They issued a statement and it duly appeared in the *Irish Workers' Voice*:

> We, the small farmers and workers of the Leitrim area, in mass meeting assembled, do hereby declare ourselves opposed to

the deportation of James Gralton from his native land and home of his birth. And, be it further resolved, that we are opposed to deportation in any form, as we are to every move made by the diabolical hand of imperialism that is still working in our land. And further we emphatically deny that James Gralton is being deported in the interest of 'public welfare' as the deportation order states, since experience has taught us that he is one of the most industrious and desirable residents in our locality, and that he is one who has given the best years of his life to the Irish national independence and revolutionary workers' movement. We therefore demand that the Minister of Justice rescind his deportation order immediately.

Worker and Labour publications at home and abroad carried the news. National dailies also. Gralton's followers canvassed their local Dáil deputies but, instead of satisfaction, they received lectures on the dangerous individual who was propagating English ideas that were contrary to the Christian principles of the majority of the people. Sligo-Leitrim Fianna Fáil T.D., Ben Maguire, told how his party based its policies on the encyclicals of Pope Leo XIII and how its members were slaves only to Christian charity.

Dublin organised a defence committee too. Prominent writers like Peadar O'Donnell, Francis Stuart, Denis Johnston, F.R. Higgins and Frank O'Connor joined it, alongside Revolutionary Workers' Groups, trade unions, unemployed organisations and assorted left-wing individuals. Hannah Sheehy-Skeffington chaired a well-attended meeting at the Rotunda on 26 February. The IRA army council announced that it would take an independent line. Many claim this amounted to little or nothing.

The deportation order expired on 5 March but on the first day of the month, members of An Garda Síochána arrived at Gralton's home to arrest him. Previously, Gralton had been thatching the roof over his bedroom and had thrown a temporary cover over it. He asked to change his clothes, went into his room and escaped through the roof. Gralton was on the run again.

Leitrim people, some of whom held no sympathy for his socialist views, housed him. A number of national organisations passed resolutions condemning the deportation order.

Peadar O'Donnell and some Dublin socialist activists came to Effernagh and discussed matters with local supporters in Gralton's house. James turned up for a while but left again. They planned an after-Mass meeting for 5 March. The parish priest, Fr Cosgrave, brought the Mass time forward and warned his congregation not to listen to the anti-God men and agents of anti-Christ from the city. Later, he approached the meeting as it began and abused those on the platform. His part-time housekeeper threw a sod at O'Donnell and, when others followed her example, the speakers abandoned the platform. They got into their cars amid cries of abuse. Protesters blocked their exit from the town. Gardaí who had been reticent earlier, now intervened and drew batons while the car reversed away. Later that day O'Donnell managed to address a meeting at Effernagh, where he criticised the clergy and muck-throwers.

Press coverage of the Drumsna incident was considerable. The pro Fianna Fáil publication, *An Phoblacht*, suggested that a secret sectarian society had orchestrated it. The *Irish Workers' Voice* blamed the local IRA. In its issue of 4 March 1933 it stated:

> The right wing of the Republican leadership has no enthusiasm for the fight on Gralton. This is clearly shown in the columns of *An Phoblacht*. The first week of the struggle it was silent. Perhaps there is here the justification that the full facts had to be verified on the spot. But last week's article approached the genuine question in literary fear and trembling. Gralton is introduced to the Republican readers as a good harmless boy whom any respectable country lady or gentleman need have no fear of supporting.

Later, the feature commented:

> But the Gralton case is the very essence of the battle now raging between the worker and farmer masses and the capitalists, of whom the Fianna Fáil Government is the representative ... The Gralton case from start to finish was a most shameful act carried out in the very early days of the Fianna Fáil regime. They bowed to the clamours of the most reactionary anti-national, anti-progressive forces, the gombeens, the ranchers and their clerical front men in Leitrim. Gralton

was among the first, possibly the first of the victims of the Fianna Fáil regime.

Gralton was a Republican, a Democrat, a Communist; the Ireland he wanted was the one that James Connolly wanted.

Gralton's Ireland was not what the people of property in Leitrim or anywhere else in the country wanted.

The clergy in Gowel again called in the Redemptorists to preach against the spread of evil ideology. The missioners praised those who had attacked the speakers in Drumsna. The Leitrim Board of Health unanimously condemned Communism. Later, it received a letter complaining about this action. It was burned. It had come from the Irish Worker' Republican Emancipation Alliance in New York.

The 'fallen state' of James Gralton was the subject of many sermons, as was the duty of the Church and State in defending people against 'Communist wolves'. Leitrim county councillors were inundated with mail, a large portion of it from the United States. They discussed the matter in May. In a long debate, most of the speakers defended the Minister's right to deport Gralton, but a few strong voices demanded a fair trial. Gralton's mother attended another meeting in July and pleaded for her son. James had written to the Council and they agreed to read his letter. It said:

I would ask you, in the interests of common decency and honesty to bring the following facts before the Council for consideration at the next meeting. Immediately after the Board of Health resolution was passed, I started on a tour of the country. I went from townland to townland and from parish to parish. I held meetings with from five to fifteen people every place I stopped, and I find that after the miserable story behind the deportation order was made known, the people everywhere resented it. As a result of this tour and those meetings I have with me now 41 resolutions condemning the attitude of the Board of Health and calling on the Government to place me on trial to answer whatever charges may be brought against me. In view of the fact that the Council has interested itself in my case, at least to the extent of inquiring into my private family affairs such as 'was my father attended by the priest previous to his death?' and in view of the further fact that the considered opinion of the Council, embodied in a resolution, is held by many to reflect the sentiment of the common people in cases such as mine, I ask the Council to comply with the wishes of the vast majority of the people of Breffni, who undoubtedly stand for fair play, and place itself on record as being opposed to secret tyranny by demanding a trial by jury for me.

James Gralton

Gralton was still stirring up trouble and the authorities took action. The Gardaí renewed their search for Leitrim's Communist son with vigour. After intensive house searching, they apprehended him in an armed raid on the house of Francis Beirne at Gorvagh on 10 August. Held overnight in Ballinamore, he was escorted to Cork jail the next morning. The authorities used Gralton's own money to purchase a ticket and at 3.30pm on 13 August 1933 the six-month-old deportation order was finally put into effect.

The *Leitrim Observer* of 19 August 1933 mentioned the deportation in its 'Pars and Points' column and commented: 'When the news spread throughout Leitrim on Saturday no one seemed to give the matter a moment's thought; business was as usual and the plain people pursued the even tenor of their way.' Its fuller coverage went:

DEPORTATION OF JAMES GRALTON

NOW ON WAY TO AMERICA

ARRESTED IN LEITRIM AND BROUGHT TO COBH

PROTEST MADE ON LINER

The Irish-American James Gralton of Gowel, Carrick-on-Shannon, was deported from Ireland on Sunday last. He was put aboard the Britannic, *which left Cobh for New York.*

James Gralton, for whose deportation an order was made by the Minister for Justice in February last and who had since been on the run, was arrested by Gardai in a house near Ballinamore early on Saturday morning.

It was alleged that he held advanced Communistic views. He built a hall for the youth of his district, which was fired into and bombed and finally burned. Inscriptions have, during the past month, been placed on public buildings in Leitrim demanding a public trial for Gralton.

After his arrest Gralton was taken to Carrick-on-Shannon and thence via Limerick to Cork, where he was lodged in the prison. At about 2.30 a.m. he was taken from the prison by Supt MacNeill, Cork, and an escort of four detectives, and motored to Cobh. He was detained at Cobh until shortly before the departure of the tender at about five o'clock. Inspector Diggins, Cobh, accompanied the party to the liner.

The Formalities

Gralton, who wore a cap, a heavy overcoat, and a red cardigan, appeared fresh, despite his long journey by motor from Leitrim. He was in good spirits and chatted with some of his escort during the trip through the harbour. He was given third-class accommodation.

The formalities connected with his departure did not occupy much time at the shore or on board the liner. His passport was in order and Supt MacNeill produced the deportation order dated 3 February, 1933.

When a Press reporter interviewed him on board the Britannic, Gralton said he felt disgusted at being shipped from his native land in this way. He had thought, he said, that he would at least have been given a trial by the Government that he supported in his own small way.

'My treatment,' he said, 'comes ill at the hands of representatives of a people who have been crying against persecution for hundreds of years.'

He said that, after he had been served with the deportation order, he endeavoured to get an interview with the Minister for Justice, but that was refused.

'I went on the run,' he added, 'because I did not want to be railroaded out of the country on the quiet. I wanted to get all the publicity possible. It is a very dangerous procedure to ship a man out of the country without the semblance of a trial.'

He said that he had received excellent treatment at the hands of the detectives and uniformed guards in whose custody he had been since his capture. His only complaint was against the action of the Government.

52

When the *Brittanica* docked in New York a reception committee met Gralton. The left-wing press interviewed him and soon he was politically active again. What happened in Ireland urged him to write to one of his tormentors in Gowel:

New York City, U.S..A.

Rev Father O Dowd,

Dear Father,
Some time ago you stated in a sermon that you had gained a 'noble victory' in Gowel; that you did not want the credit for that victory, but shared it with Father O'Donoghue of Carrick-on-Shannon.

Now let us analyse this supposed victory of yours, and see what is noble about it. Let us see if there is anything connected with it that a decent-minded man might be proud of.

You started out on a crusade against Communism by demanding that the Pearse-Connolly Hall be handed over to you. You knew the cash that paid for the material was given to the people of Gowel by P. Rowley, J.P. Farrell and myself.

You also know that the labour was furnished free, and that it belonged to all the people of the area, irrespective of religious or political affiliations. But despite this you, with the greedy gall of a treacherous grabber, tried to get it into your own clutches. I put it to you straight, Father: is there anything noble about this? The people answered 'No' when they voted unanimously that you could not have it.

The hall was in my name; you knew from experience that you could not frighten me into transferring it to you, so you organised a gang to murder me. You bullied little children, manhandled old women, lied scandalously about Russia, blathered ignorantly about Mexico and Spain, and incited young lads into becoming criminals by firing into the hall.

You did all these things because you could not close it, although you bragged Sunday after Sunday that 95% of the people were behind you. You are a noble man, Father; so is Father O'Donoghue for that matter. He went to Dublin but he did not succeed in having me expelled from the Drumsna Fianna Fáil club. Sure, he managed to have a few pounds relief money put at your disposal. By the way, Father, how many lads came to you cap in hand for the job? Answer: none.

The last act (perhaps) in your 'noble victory' was the deportation order, but you were only the local stool-pigeon. By this time 95% of the people were with you, if your word is to be taken for it. Still with all these people behind you [you] did not come out in the open, but carried on like a thief in the night, and with the connivance of the government tried to railroad me quietly out of the country.

Here again your 'noble victory' went astray, for it was only after six months, and after the case had got considerable publicity on two continents, that I was finally placed aboard ship.

You want to share this 'victory' of the Irish capitalists and the British imperialists with Father O'Donoghue, but why stop here? Surely you got assistance from other sources? How about the Executive Council, the Knights of Columbanus, the firing squad, the petrol gang, the Standard, the gombeen press, and cads like Andrew Mooney and MacMorrow N.T. P.C. [National Teacher. Peace Commissioner]? And why forget the CID and the spies? In short, the whole motley crew who helped Buckshot Forster [W.E., the British Chief Secretary who introduced Coercion Bill – The Protection of Person and Property Bill, 1880], Bloody Balfour [Arthur James. British Prime Minister, 1902-05] and the 'Tans [Black and Tans] to their 'noble victory'.

Father, another such 'victory' and you will be of no further use to the criminal ruling class in Ireland (in Gowel at any rate) – even the cloak of religion can no longer cover the Imperialist hooligan that hides behind it.

Yours very sincerely,
James Gralton

Gralton did not allow bitterness to curb his activities, however. He stood for the Communist Party in the next New York Borough elections but failed to win a seat. Workers' Clubs with which he had been associated before in the United States benefited from his renewed interest in improving them. Those thinking of opening new branches in other cities found a willing helper in Gralton too. In partnership with a Longford emigrant, he started up a tea and eggs business. This fared reasonably well until World War II. Petrol shortages and huge running costs brought the business down and Gralton became unemployed. His stomach complaint was getting worse when he began working again with WOV, a New York radio station. At 59 years of age he married Bessie Cronnogue from Drumsna, but died in Bellvue Hospital a short while later, on 29 December 1945.

Peadar O'Donnell, who figured in the events of the time once said, 'We are not a priest-ridden society, but we have a society-ridden clergy'. In rural Ireland of the 1930s and 1940s the local priest drove in one of the few cars about. Most of his flock fawned over him. One family tried to out-do another in bestowing favours on him. Some right-thinking priests found this distasteful but many revelled in it. Only an odd lay person had the backbone to speak out against clerical-induced injustices. It is difficult today to appreciate how remarkable was James Gralton's stand. The very suggestion of Communism in south Leitrim must have caused enormous apprehension. Succeeding in building up a considerable following for its ideology was an incredible achievement. James Gralton was, without question, a leader.

POSTSCRIPT

The 'Gralton Affair' was not a popular subject in a self-conscious Ireland that was attempting to shake off a number of alleged Church-State embarrassments in the late 1940s and 1950s. A Communist Party of Ireland emerged in November 1921 after Roderick Connolly took charge of the Socialist Party of Ireland. This movement, of which Peadar O'Donnell and Liam O'Flaherty were members, attracted little support and gave way to James Larkin's Irish Workers' League. In 1933, a few months after James Gralton's deportation, the Revolutionary Workers' Group and the Workers' Party of Ireland re-established the Communist Party.

Almost 40 years after James Gralton's death, a few issues of a socialist magazine called *Gralton* appeared. In it, Brian Trench explained why the name was chosen. He outlined the events recorded above and completed his feature by saying:

> Above all ... Gralton's name represents a challenge to established authority, a call for people to take their fate into their own hands, an imaginative application of socialist ideas in a difficult environment, and a recognition that wherever socialists happen to be, that's where they should be active. For all that, and more, he deserves to be remembered.

In 1986, a Gralton Commemoration Committee celebrated the centenary of his birth. A ballad by Martin McGoldrick from Sligo, sung to the air of *The Flower of Sweet Strabane* perpetuates the man and his deportation:

They hunted you Jim Gralton from your Father's ancient home,
And shipped you like their cattle across the ocean foam,
Those rich men are so holy, they decreed that you must fly,
So in their Christian charity you are left alone to die.

Were you of the robber classes that live by loot and gain,
Upon the 'sweated masses' they would crave to remain,
Had you ten thousand acres and blood stain in every field,
The empire and its herdsmen to your slightest whim would
    yield.

Had you cars and bullock ranches, and herds with spies to
    boot,
The Church and State behind you, they would help to guard
    your loot,
Or the Lord of crumbling hovels, or the boss of sweated slaves,
You would now be Sir James Gralton among a pack of robber
    knaves.

But you craved not for those vices, you were loyal to your
    kind,
You left your fellow workers in body and in mind,
You did serve your fellow worker who long wasted flesh and
    bone,
To enrich and idle robber, you nerve him seize his own.

For this you are called unholy and for this you must fly,
From your land and feeble mother you must leave me here to
    die,
Since the property is so sacred, must apply along to things,
That was seized by blood and plunder, to enrich great Lords
    and Kings.

But the workers day is coming though another come for me,
The dawn of Ireland's freedom on earth I never shall see,
But I will rejoice in glory in a land beyond the grave,
When Ireland and the world has freed the fettered slave.

THE TAILOR AND ANSTY

Statutes dealing with censorship of literature in Ireland have always been clumsy. Section 42 of The Customs Consolidation Act of 1876 set out the procedure whereby police could receive a search warrant from any magistrate who received, under oath, a complaint concerning purchase of an obscene article. The vendor was then called to defend himself. If he was unable to justify the sale, he could appeal or hand over the condemned goods for destruction. The trouble was, the statute did not define 'obscenity'. The situation became more complicated when Saorstát Éireann, the Irish Free State, emerged in 1922. Much of the material considered offensive was imported, so action could be taken only against distributors, newsagents and booksellers. Watchful groups emerged from time to time. The Irish Vigilance Association (1911) brought assorted pressures to bear, issued circulars, wrote to newspaper editors and generally kept a watchful eye on things. The government passed a Censorship of Films Act in 1923, but a committee still sat on the legal literature issue. British Sunday newspapers were its main target. Not until 16 July 1929 was The Censorship of Publications Bill passed. Provision for appeal was added in February 1947. In the meantime, neutrality during a world war presented new censorial difficulties.

Censorship on grounds of indecency, however, remained a problem. It reared a somewhat ridiculous head in the case of a book about an old couple who lived near beautiful Gougane Barra in west Cork.

On 26 December 1863, Timothy Buckley was born in Lonnachán, Knockaunavona, in the County Kerry parish of Kilgarvin. His father, Padraig, had a 60-acre farm and grazing rights with two others on 300 acres of mountain commonage. Timothy had ten brothers and two sisters and was himself a seventh son. *'Mise an seacht mac, i ndiaidh a chéile gan aon bhriseadh,' aduirt sé.* A seventh son often 'had the cure' for

57

many ailments. Poor Timothy, on the contrary, developed infantile paralysis when only nine years of age. As a result, his right leg, from knee to toe, stopped growing. When he got older, therefore, he used a crutch. At thirteen years of age, he began a five year apprenticeship to a tailor in Kenmare. When this was over, he worked at his trade in Killarney, Tralee, Mallow and Cork, where he spent four years. Then he went to Youghal. Despite his handicap, he managed to travel to Dublin and to Scotland. Finally, he returned home and married Anastasia McCarthy on 3 June 1906 in the small church at Gougane Barra. They lived at Ansty's place in Gearnapeaka near Lough Gougane Barra.

Nicknamed The Tailor because that was his trade, Buckley would promise to 'build a suit' for a client, but would spend longer talking than stitching. So he did not have many customers. He was a brilliant Irish language conversationalist. Because of his travelling, however, he spoke English fluently too and could turn a phrase better than a trouser flap. Soon he matured into an accomplished *seanachai* – more a folk raconteur, perhaps, because he had a winning technique. He loved people and relished nothing better than tracing a family's ancestors or history. Listening to events from their past or consoling them in their troubles caused him no hardship either. Always, he praised his neighbours for their capacity to enjoy themselves and for their wealth of lore. From what seemed a mere casual witticism, he could develop a story enriched with old sayings, wise advice and anecdotal asides.

The Tailor lived life to its most vibrant in his new environment described by himself as being 'in the townland of Gearnapeaka in the district of Inchigeela, in the parish of Iveleary, in the barony of West Muskerry, in the County of Cork'. His handicap grew worse and prevented him from leaving his home. His wife Anastasia, or Ansty, 'his bitter half', was his opposite. The Tailor was an optimist, Ansty found fault with everything. Eric Cross (*The Tailor and Ansty*, Cork and Dublin 1985) elaborates: 'The Tailor sits, Silenus-like, upon his butter-box by the side of the fire, with fun and interest dancing in his eyes. Ansty wanders in and out of the house, broom in hand, hair awry, looking like one of the Furies and acting as an antithetical chorus to The Tailor's view of life.'

The Tailor passed on a considerable corpus of his stories to Sean Ó Cróinín a collector employed by the Irish Folklore Commission. Over three weeks he related his rich store of folklore. Sean recorded it on an Ediphone and also transcribed it. Frank O'Connor, who described The Tailor as a rural Dr Johnson, often visited the Buckleys in their mountainy cottage. He remembered The Tailor as 'a crippled little Kerryman with soft, round, rosy cheeks ... and two mischievous baby eyes'. He quoted his comment on the rise of Fascism: 'There wouldn't be half of this trouble if more people fell to breeding.' That was The Tailor. Earthy, even coarse!

When O'Connor's translation of Brian Merriman's *The Midnight Court* was banned, The Tailor fumed, 'You can't know a man and only know half of him. If you want to know a man you must know the whole of him, and it should never have been banned – all of it must go in.' A young Dublin priest, Fr Traynor visited. Seamus Murphy, the Cork sculptor, too. The American journalist Ripley called to them and to another house in the area. Ansty criticised the neighbours for giving 'Ruppeley nathing but ould vine to drink; no fuishkey at aaal!'

From Newry, Co. Down, Eric Cross became a regular caller for close on 40 years. An English-educated scientist, he had invented synthetic marble and converted bicycle-spokes into knitting needles in the aftermath of World War II when the genuine articles were scarce and expensive. Friends of The Tailor and Ansty urged Cross to type a memoir, which he did. Under Seán Ó Faoláin's editorship, *The Bell* serialised it. People said it was too brief, so in 1942, Cross published a book of short stories based on what he saw of and heard from The Tailor and Ansty. *The Sunday Independent* gave it an enthusiastic review. Frank O'Connor felt it preserved the warmth and humanity of the couple, but blamed himself for not realising that 'to all good Irishmen a book is anathema' (*Leinster, Munster and Connaught,* London undated).

Cross commented, 'The publication roused the rancour of that small but active body of pharisees which exist in every country, driving them to ugly words and deeds and the banning of the book.' On 2 October 1942, the Censorship Board banned it as being, in its general tendency, indecent.

CONTROVERSY RAGED. The Tailor and his wife were not unduly excited, mainly because The Tailor became seriously ill. Sick or not, three priests came to his house and forced him to kneel before the fireside and throw a copy of his book into the flames. Ansty took to her usual complaining. Her main concern was the fact that it was a waste of eight and sixpence, the price of the volume.

Some self-righteous people and others who merely lacked backbone avoided the household that once played host to dozens of callers. Eminent people who had frequented the place and revelled in the earthy chatter of the couple stayed silent.

During a four-day Senate debate on a Censorship of Publications motion, the book had a gallant defender in Sir John Keane. It had strident adversaries too. Frank O'Connor described the reading of Senators' speeches as being like 'a long, slow swim through a sewage bed'. The official report of the Senate debate on 18 November 1942 reads:

Sir John Keane: I move – that, in the opinion of Seanad Éireann, the Censorship of Publications Board appointed by the Minister for Justice under the Censorship of Publications Act, 1929, has ceased to retain public confidence, and that steps should be taken by the Minister to reconstitute the board.

It is with no little hesitation I propose this motion. I know the subject is not popular and my first inclination would be to do as many others are doing about this matter, to adopt an attitude of cynical indifference, to say in my own mind that the whole thing is ridiculous and to be satisfied if

I, personally, and my friends were not interfered with. I do not think that is adequate. I think there is a big principle involved in this, and I feel it my duty as a public representative, after 13 years of operation of this Act, to ask the House to consider where the country stands in this whole matter. I am not challenging the main principle of censorship. The battle was fought and lost 13 years ago. My views are on record for those who wish to read them. I contested the proposal resolutely in its entirety. I said the thing was not workable and that the methods employed across the water were quite adequate to safeguard the morals of our country as regards reading. However, Parliament thought differently, and we have had this Bill, which has now been in operation for 13 years. I am striving for the legal safeguards that were embodied in that measure.

After all, we are still governed by the rule of the law, and where one has reason to believe that the rule of law is being disregarded there is a public duty to call attention to the fact. What were the safeguards which were introduced into this measure? They were mainly two. I shall read from Section 6 of the Act:

> Whenever a complaint is duly made under this Act to the Minister to the effect that a book or a particular edition of a book is indecent or obscene or advocates the unnatural prevention of conception or the procurement of abortion or miscarriage or the use of any method, treatment or appliance for the purpose of such prevention or such procurement, the Minister may refer such complaint to the Board.

I have to deal fairly frankly with this whole subject. After all, we are all aware of the facts of life, and unless I deal frankly with the subject it is quite impossible for me to make my case. Senators have to read that section in connection with the definition. There was a great deal of controversy about the definition, and finally and, I think, somewhat reluctantly, the government conceded this defintion of 'indecency'.

The word 'indecency' shall be construed as including suggestive of, or inciting to sexual immorality or unnatural vice or likely in any other similar way to corrupt or deprave.

61

It is in the light of these safeguards that I wish the House to examine what has happened. In that connection it is appropriate to quote certain passages, and more particularly passages containing what the Minister said, from the debate which took place when the Bill was being passed. In a court of law what the Minister said could not be quoted, but I take it that there is general agreement that this House is acting more as a court of equity. The Minister said in the debate on the Bill:

> As to the general principles on which the board of censors should act ... there must be general agreement amongst all reasonable and intelligent men. A book can be fairly condemned only when, in its whole course, it makes for evil, when its tenor is bad, when, in some important part of it, it is indecent, when – I might put it this way – it is systematically indecent.

On the next page, the Minister, adopting the jargon of his profession, says:

> To my mind, that is a great, broad, clear distinction, a distinction which, as I said before, I believe all intelligent, thinking men will agree exists. To sum it up in two short phrases: a book to be condemned must *ex professo* be immoral; it cannot be condemned if it is immoral merely *obiter*.

I hope the House understands that.

Mr M. Hayes: The Senator will have to get a grind in more than Irish.

Sir John Keane: Senator Tierney took a very active part in the debate on this Bill 13 years ago. He said in that debate: 'I am very much afraid that the result of this section' – he was, I think, dealing with Section 6, but I have been unable to make sure of that from the context: '– will be that, under the authority of this Dáil, a list of prohibited books will be produced which will make a laughing stock of this country.'

The Senator had certainly prophetic vision when he made that statement.

... I come to the book entitled *The Tailor and Ansty*. This book apparently aroused a great deal of interest – more interest than did other books which, I think, are far more deserving of interest. It is a book dealing with local country life. It contains the sayings of country folk in rather a remote part of County Cork, the sayings of an unsophisticated but, nevertheless, rather inter-esting and racy couple – The Tailor and his wife, Ansty. Its banning has aroused more indignation, I think, on the part of those who are interested in the domestic literature and genius of our people than on the part of those interested in that of the wider world. If I am not wrongly informed, those with Gaelic sympathies raised their voices for the first time in opposition to and in condemnation of this censorship. They did that on account of this book.

I do not want to hide anything from the House. The book is somewhat Rabelaisian in character. I understand – many people know this better than I do – that country folk, talking around the fireside, are somewhat frank and, perhaps, coarse in their expressions. I propose to read you certain passages from this book, which I feel entitled to do in order to make my case. I do not want the Seanad to be under any delusion as to what the book is about. Unfortunately, some Senators cannot get it. I got it, and I could have got as many copies as I wanted. If any body wants to get a censored book, there is no trouble in getting it; I do not mean any ordinary plain person, but anybody who knows the way about. Here is a sample. The Tailor had not seen much of the world; he did not want to see much of the world, because he knew life better than those educated people. But they persuaded him to go to a cinema in Cork, and these are his comments:

(Here the Senator quoted from the book.)

[The portion of the book describes the visit to the Astoria and includes amusing comments on the newsreel and the trailer before the feature film. The portion that could not be written into the official record is probably that describing the Tailor's reaction to a 'shy love scene':

'Hould her! Hould her! You'd think by the shaping of her that she did not like it, but I tell you that they are all that way in the

beginning. It is a way they have of letting on that they don't like it, when all the time they like it as a donkey likes strawberries ... Thon amon dieu! Man, if I was twenty years younger, I'd come up and give you lessons.'

Sir John Keane then remarked, 'I do not suppose the Censor minded that. It goes on' – and the official record tells that he quoted more. Probably the section where The Tailor passed unfavourable comment on the heroine, but praised her mother: 'A nice class of a woman ... a man... could knock a winter out of her comfortably.'

He thought the leading ladies were a bit on the thin side:
'They need a basinfull of stirabout and thick milk a few times a day, and then they would be all right.'

Yet one of them was too fat for his liking:
'A devil of a great pounder of a woman. She'd make a handy door for a car-house. She'd stifle you in the bed. People think that fat women are warm. I tell you they are not. They make a damn great tunnel in the bed and a man may as well be sleeping in a gully.'

Back to the official record and Sir John]:

I am not reading this in order to call forth amusement. I am reading them out seriously, as samples which you should hear, and on which you should form your own judgement. There is another passage, but it is only incidental, where they make fun of modern education because they find that some of the younger people, even though they are married, do not know the difference between a cow and a bull. I do not imagine that can be the offending passage. I fancy this is the offending passage here, but, according to the definition in the Act, a book, in order to be censored, must be in its general tendency indecent. The first passage I read was on page 54* [see author's note at end of chapter].

Professor Magennis: Would the Senator read the rest of that reference? I think I am entitled to ask, if he quotes a passage, that he should quote it in its entirety.

Sir John Keane: Unfortunately, I thought I made a note on the back of the cover, but I find that I did not. I am only too anxious to read it. Could the Senator tell me what page it is on? I cannot find it, and I do not want to take up the time of the House.

Professor Magennis: I suggest to the Chairman that, before Senator Sir John Keane reads the remainder of the passage, an instruction should be given to the official reporters not to record it. Otherwise, we shall have some of the vilest obscenity in our records, and the Official Reports can be bought for a few pence.

Mr M. Hayes: I should like to be clear as to what are to be the rules of debate on this matter. I can understand the anxiety of Professor Magennis that the passage be read in its entirety, but it would be an extraordinary thing if we were to adopt the rule that we must hear the whole of them in all their obscenity.

Professor Magennis: What I submit is this: the only defence that can be made by the censorship is to give the public an idea of what the thing is, in its real and full character. I would not foul my lips nor defile the ears of this House by quoting the passage in its entirety, and I had no anticipation that Senator Sir John Keane would quote from the book, but when he does quote and omits what is the gravamen of the offence, then I am entitled to draw the attention of the House to the fact that the quotation is garbled, and it is for the chairman to decide on the dilemma which Senator Hayes has properly pointed out. I do not want it recorded. Some fig-leaf language can be used to describe it, but it must not be referred to merely as a piece of harmless, if coarse, jocosity.

Mr Goulding: I happen to have read this book, and I certainly object to some of its passages being read out in this House. They are generally obscene and I would be very loath to sit here and listen to them.

Sir John Keane: I am in the hands of the Chairman. If the Chairman rules, I will ask the Committee of Privileges to sit in regard to the matter. I consider that I am perfectly entitled to quote from a book which has been censored and put the facts before the House.

Cathaoirleach: The Senator is entitled to quote.

Sir John Keane: I will read the passage to which I have referred.

(Again, the Senator quoted from the book.)

[Perhaps it was The Tailor's description of two country caubogues in a boarding house in Mallow who slept in the one bed and who did not know what the chamber pots under the bed were. Fionn Mac Cumhaill's teacups? No! Nightcaps, they concluded.]

Professor Magennis: I would now ask Senator Sir John Keane if he will first read the next passage to himself.

Sir John Keane: I will go on until Senator Magennis tells me to stop.

Professor Magennis: The Senator is now trying to put upon me the responsibility for having this stuff read out and put in the Official Reports. I am asking, in the interests of public decency, that he should read the next paragraph to himself before he inflicts it on the House.

Sir John Keane: I have considered all the implications of this. I consider that, if we are going to be put under what I suggest is a literary Gestapo, we are entitled to know the facts.

Cathaoirleach: The Senator might use discretion as to the quotations. There is Ministerial responsibility for the Board, and the Senator may employ quotations to illustrate the arguments for the motion.

Sir John Keane: I know; I was going to deal with that point. Responsibility is on the Minister and I was going to deal with that point later on. The Minister takes responsibility, and that is why the matter is raised here.

Professor Magennis: On a point of explanation, the Senator has tried to fix responsibility on me because I said that the only defence for the censorship would be to make the public acquainted with the contents of the book. I suggested to him that to leave off with a quotation which, though coarse, was comparatively harmless, was to give a wrong impression, and then he said that if I demanded it he would read it. That, I submit, is to put the responsibility for the reading of it on me, and I have appealed to him to read the passage to himself and use his own discretion.

Cathaoirleach: The Chair's concern is with the terms of the motion on the Order Paper of the House.

(Sir John Keane quoted from the book.)

[Might it have been a verse or two of The Tailor's song?

> *When summer's tasks were over and when winter's rains did spout,*
> *In search of a sweetheart I instantly set out.*
> *Down to a cottage that I had long in view,*
> *For I got a zeal for courting –*
>   *I had nothing else to do!*
>
> *I warmly saluted her, and down by her I sat,*
> *For a time we were discoursing and giving each other chat.*
> *She liked my conversation till something else got in her view,*
> *There she got a zeal for courting too –*
>   *She had nothing else to do!]*

Cathaoirleach: I presume the Senator does not intend to read the whole book?

Sir John Keane: Not the whole book, but I do not want to be accused by Senator Magennis of distorting or suppressing anything.

Padraic Ó Maille: I think the Censor was a public benefactor in stopping that kind of rubbish.

Sir John Keane: That is a matter of opinion. We are each entitled to have our own opinion, and I would ask the Senator to have respect for my sincere and honest opinion. It may be misguided but –

Professor Magennis: There is a part of the constitution which guarantees full liberty of expression but there is an express proviso with regard to the safeguarding of public morals.

Sir John Keane: But, is not the book in circulation for quite a long time? A number of people have read it. I am sure the

Senator would not read it. I take it that the Senator is contending that I should not be allowed to read from a banned book. I think that is an entirely unconstitutional argument.

Mr M. Hayes: These interruptions are not fair, Sir.

Professor Magennis: It is not fair to the House to have this book read and put in the Official Reports, where it can be bought and read by members of the public.

Sir John Keane: That is for the House to say.

Cathaoirleach: The Senator must be allowed to proceed. I will consider the action I should take on the other matter.

Sir John Keane: Thank you, Sir. I am entitled to go on until I am ruled out of order. There is a further passage – the last one I intend to read from this book – and I am entitled to read it.

(The Senator quoted from the book.)

[Coarse, degrading comments on women, perhaps? The Tailor says:

> *Women are like cattle. There are some of them will breed for you if you only look at them, and some of them go for the 'pusher' time and time again and won't have any calf.*

And later,

> *... the cow is the hub of the household. You couldn't think of having a pig unless you kept a cow first. If you were to come here you would first have to get a wife, and then a cow. And the first thing you would have to look for in the wife would be if she was a good milker. You might get the cow as dowry with the wife, and you could not do better, unless there was a bit of money as well. If you had the cow, you could live without the wife, but if you had not the cow you would not be able to live at all.]*

I do not think there is anything more in it unless the Senator is interested.

Professor Magennis: If the Senator would like me to answer him –

Mr M. Hayes: I think, Sir, we have had enough.

Professor Magennis rose.

Cathaoirleach: On a point of order?

Sir John Keane: I can assure the House that I have plenty of time.

Mr M. Hayes: We have had enough.

Sir John Keane: (Quotes from the book.)

[Perhaps it was The Tailor's story:

I remember a story of the time when they first used 'the enemy' in this country. There was a man, by the name of Tim Donovan, sent for the doctor. The doctor came and had to operate on him in this way, for he was costive. When the operation was over he asked Jim, 'How are you feeling now, Jim?' 'I don't know how I am,' answered Jim, 'but do you know, doctor, I think that you may have a queer sense of fun. I like fun myself as well as any man living, but sticking a kippin (stick) up a man's backside is no fun at all in my meaning of the word.'

Or maybe the incident when The Tailor and a friend looked for a pub where they could 'have a "dog's leg" and anchor there?']

Mr M. Hayes: We have had enough of this, Sir.

Cathaoirleach: I suggest that the House has heard sufficient quotations.

Mr M. Hayes: Hear Hear!

On 2 December Professor Magennis spoke at length.

There were other speeches. On 9 December, Mr O'Dwyer said:

Mr O'Dwyer: I wish to add my voice in opposition to the motion. I am surprised that such a motion should have been brought forward. In moving it Senator Sir John Keane quoted a certain book which has recently come under public notice, *The Tailor and Ansty*. He read out certain passages in an effort to prove the Censorship Board was wrong in banning the book, but I think it was clear that the passages he quoted justified the banning of the book for all time. Other books have been quoted here in support of the motion, but the quotations again showed that the Censorship Board acted perfectly properly in banning them. I think that Senator Sir John Keane has made the best case for the existence of the Censorship Board, and has shown how necessary is its vigilance. The passages he read from *The Tailor and Ansty* were clearly immoral. What was worse, they did not form part of the story at all but were simply tacked on for the obscenity. Clearly, the motive of the writer was to introduce those topics for the sake of gain, the basest of all motives, and that is the book which the Senator cited in support of his motion. I was very surprised at that. The point was also made that 1,600 books had been banned, and that it could be possible that the board was not right in all cases. I cannot imagine any board, after reading the quotations cited by Senator Sir John Keane, failing to condemn the book containing them. I dare say that a single passage would be quite sufficient to show the general trend of the book. A great number of the books I heard about recommended the adoption of forbidden practices, and in that case there should be no hesitation in stopping their circulation. I would like to deal with what I think is the real motive behind this opposition to the censorship. I imagine that the basis of it is the defence of the liberty of the individual – the right of the individual to read whatever books he thinks fit, and the right of the author and printer to publish what they consider fit. I need not remind the House that in any Christian or civilised community there is limit to the liberty of the individual. During the year I understand that the mover sponsored another motion relating to betting shops and their suppression. As a matter of fact, I think he was right in that, and I would be glad to support him, but I ask him if he thinks that betting shops would do more harm than the free dissemination of this evil literature which he favours? Does the Senator think that the betting shops would cause more unhappy lives?

Sir John Keane: I certainly do.

Mr O'Dwyer: That is extraordinary, and it is not in accordance with the facts as seen in the outside world. The effects of the betting shops are comparatively restricted, the effects of evil literature are more widespread and terrible. No individual, I say, can claim unbounded liberty to do what he likes. If a journal or a book were to be published advocating the overthrow of the Government by force or anything like that, I am sure the Senator would be the first to call for its suppression. I consider that such a book would not be more deadly than the books which this motion advocated. We must examine the idea disseminated through evil literature. Is it not a crime as old as humanity itself? I hold the Censorship Board is doing good work in endeavouring to suppress immoral publications. Senator Sir John Keane argues that it does no harm to allow those books to be printed and circulated, because nobody need bother to buy or read them, and that they will do no harm to the ordinary person. We must also consider that propaganda from the belligerent nations. That is because they know that these things have an effect on people when they are reiterated often enough. When that is the case with war propaganda, the effect must be still greater if you have evil literature harping all the time on obscenity. It is not a question of *The Tailor and Ansty* or of any of these new books. It is more than that. We have not the exact figures but undoubtedly it is a fact that much evil literature has been imported in, not single books alone, but periodicals, weekly or otherwise, from England and foreign countries. They have been coming here for years and, through libraries, circulating to the most remote parts. As Senator Ó Buachalla explained, I saw some that came before the committee set up to inquire into the matter. We saw awful examples of the evil stuff that is being disseminated throughout the country. Is it the object of the mover of this motion to allow that to continue unchecked?

Senator The McGillycuddy said that it was the duty of the minority in this respect to obey the laws of the majority, but I do not really see how it is a question of minority or majority. It is a question which is as old as humanity itself, and concerns every religion and every race. I do not think there has been any difference up to the present between any of the Christian churches or any sections of the people on this question.

Senator Sir John Keane has done good service to the country in raising it, because for the first time it will show the people what we are up against. It is well that we should face it and see where we stand in this conflict. We know that conditions in the outside world are very bad at the moment. In Europe, America and all countries there is an increasing tendency towards immorality and lawlessness. The literature from these countries portrays the lawlessness and degeneracy into which the masses of people there have sunk. It is by such literature they are endeavouring to destroy the youth of this country, just as the youth of these other countries have been destroyed by evil literature.

The purpose of this literature is clear. Today the Government have to meet another danger, that of foreign invasion. Hundreds of thousands of our people are watching along the coast and are ready to lay down their lives to prevent invasion. There is even a greater danger confronting us, the danger of this tide of immorality which is pervading the whole world. It is the duty of the Government to defend the virtue of the Irish people against the immoral literature that threatened to overwhelm it. If these modern ideas, as I call them, got a hold, the virtue of the whole Irish race would be in danger. It is a grave question and we have to face it. I do not doubt that there are many who will laugh at that statement, but jeers and sneers matter little where the souls of our people are at stake. It is a duty of the government not to do away with the censorship, but to extend its powers so that our country is made safe, as far as it is possible to make it. The censorship must be maintained, but it needs to be strengthened. I believe that the forces of order should be called in to help the censorship. That is necessary if evil literature is to be stopped from permeating the whole country by various circulating libraries. County Council libraries see that the books are censored, but these other libraries are free to do what they like. Along with the Censorship Board, we should have the Civic Guards, and other agencies of the Government, to see that the circulation of the books, periodicals and journals I am referring to is stopped. The true answer to the motion before the house would be to have censorship strengthened.

Mr O'Callaghan: I represent a certain section of the public in this House. I have a certain amount of contact with the people I represent, and I have been careful to ascertain the views and wishes of those people during the past few weeks. I find that there is 99% agreement amongst them regarding this motion. I find, too, that, since Senator Sir John Keane tabled this motion, he has lost caste in the country. The people are asking what manner of man he is. I considered Senator Sir John Keane a very admirable member of this House, and I am sorry to see him losing caste as he, undoubtedly, has done in connection with this motion. The 'Tailor' and 'Ansty' are supposed to belong to a remote district in the County of Cork. I understand that they are supposed to typify the people in that area as regards their sayings and feelings. I know that locality fairly well and I resent very much, and the people of that locality resent very much, being put on the level of the 'Tailor' and 'Ansty.' It is a pity that clever writers such as have been quoted in this House – no doubt, they are clever – do not stick more closely to the rules of decency. They have a great opportunity to uplift the people but, judging by their books, they tend more to deprave the people.

Mr Foran: I never heard such undiluted bilge as the Senator quoted from *The Tailor and Ansty.* I have very considerable experience in connection with a mental hospital in this city. In these asylums, one meets a large number of 'Tailors' and 'Anstys'. There is a fertile field there for people who want to commercialise filth. But the people there are under control.

Unfortunately, there is an odd one abroad and he is a source of wealth and profit to people who wish to dish up this sort of stuff. I should not like to be the means of spreading propaganda for that kind of stuff. Senator Sir John Keane has not done so. That book is, I am sure, a bestseller now, owing to the attention which it got in this House. If it had not been for the attention given to it here, it would have been a 'flop'. I have never read it, although there are ways and means as Senator Keane suggested, of getting these books. That is all very well for hard-baked individuals like Senator Sir John Keane and myself. We are beyond the age when that kind of thing could have any influence upon us. But we have a responsibility to the young and the immature mind. We should not make that kind of filth available to the young people, at least until they have arrived at the age of maturity when they can appreciate, or otherwise, the value of these things. We all know the desperate and terrible effect that a boy or girl, who is mentally affected in that way, can have in a school. Parents dread them, but how much more disastrous can these books be if they remain easily available to young people ... We should not be prepared to hand over to any authority or body the power to curtail it. Certainly, we do right in trying to prevent young people having easy access to the filth and bilge which we had quoted in this House. An astute writer or publisher can always make a book a bestseller when action has been taken, such as has been in this House, calling attention to it. A certain very well-known man who did not need publicity got tremendous publicity through the action of the Lord Chamberlain when he introduced the word 'bloody' into one of his books and it was held up. It gave him a great boost.

GEORGE BERNARD SHAW would have been pleased with Mr Foran's finale! There were other objectors to the book. Senator Seán Goulding was utterly shocked. Senator Liam Ó Buachalla urged stronger powers for the Censorship Board. Senator Desmond FitzGerald uttered some sense when he said that, if he were on the Board and had to read 'all that mass of print' he would have felt called upon to censor most of the 16,000 books published in Britain each year. 'Not merely are [they] a waste of time,' he said 'but the reading of them has a corrosive effect upon the mind.'

There is no need to comment on that Senate debate. Some of its pious utterings are remarkable, if not almost incredible. The year was 1942, but later in this book another furore over an American play took place. *The Rose Tattoo* affair occurred 15 years after the banning of *The Tailor and Ansty*. Attitudes to straight talk about sex changed slowly in Ireland!

Frank O'Connor, elaborationg on the swim through sewage, poignantly wrote: 'Nobody who does not know the Irish countryside can realise the extent of the tragedy which descended on that old couple at the end of their days.' When people are old as we are there is little more the world can do to them,' The Tailor said, masking his grief with philosophy. 'But Anstey *(sic)* had never learned philosophy. You could see the old woman was eating her heart out.'

A member of An Garda Síochána cycled from Ballingeary each week to check on the couple and to discourage hooliganism. Frank O'Connor visited and, when he was about to leave, discovered that some blackguards had forced a length of a tree bough between the latch and the lintel of the door, making it impossible to open. Ansty became agitated but The Tailor consoled her. Young Jackie Buckley squeezed himself through a small window to free the door.

The Tailor died on 21 April 1945 and neighbours who had shunned him called to sympatise with Ansty. She complained about the amount of her tea they drank. Sadly, she recalled all the chastising she had done on her man for reddening his pipe in bed. A little proudly she remarked that there would be great chatting in heaven that night. Some men who sat around the fire had a more serious complaint: as The Tailor passed away, Guard Hoare, his friend, was cycling out again from Ballingeary with a bottle of whiskey.

Ansty finished her days in Cork District Hospital. She was 40 miles from Gearnapeaka but she thought she was still at home. She asked visitors if anyone was 'standing to the cow', the question she had asked The Tailor so often.

POSTSCRIPT

The Tailor and Ansty ran out of print and became a collector's item before it was unbanned. A second edition appeared in 1963. Frank O'Connor wrote an introduction which described Ansty's early beauty and her later attitude on meeting a man:

> She wanted to know at once whether or not you were married and how many children you had, and if you failed to come up to her standards of sexual performance offered you 'the loan of my ould shtal's breeches'. To her, all men were 'shtals' – stallions – including her husband, and it offended her nice sense of propriety to see a young woman who was not in the way of breeding. She and The Tailor both regarded sexual relations as the most entertaining subject for general conversation; a feature of life in Irish-speaking Ireland even in my youth, but which began to die out the moment English became the accepted language.

As The Tailor would say, 'the world's gone alabastery'.

*AUTHOR'S NOTE, p.54. In the main, the passage, quoting The Tailor, reads:

'What started it was a woman who walked down the road the other day while I was standing to the cow. When she saw the cow, I declare to God didn't she ask me if it was a bull or a cow ...'

'A bull or a cow! Glory be! Asked if it was a bull or a cow!' echoes the chorus (Ansty).

'and she wasn't a young woman either, and she was married by the ring on her finger –'

'Married – and asked "Was it a bull or a cow?"' Ansty is stunned with amazement. The joke seems too absurd even for her. 'Hould, you divil!' she hurls at The Tailor to check his extravagance. 'It passes all belief.'

'– and she had been drinking milk all her life – and, man-alive! she didn't know the difference between a bull and a cow ...'

WHISKEY, YOU'RE THE DIVIL!

First licensed in 1757 as The Brusna Distillery, Locke's Distillery, in Kilbeggan, Co. Westmeath produced whiskey for over 200 years. The river that drove the wheel for grinding is now called the Brosna. In the third quarter of the nineteenth century, John Locke began expanding the business. This was in the face of a slump in the whiskey trade. His wife, Mary Anne, and sons, John E. and James H., continued with this progress until annual output exceeded 150,000 gallons. In 1893 the business became incorporated under the Companies Act but the Locke family held control. For some years, the company thrived, but a slump during the depression that followed the Great War of 1914-18 triggered its decline.

Locke's closed in 1924 but re-opened in 1931. The deterioration continued throughout another war and its aftermath. During World War II, there were rumours of a 'black market' trade operating from within the distillery. By 1947, James Harvey Locke and his wife Mary were dead. Their daughters, Mary Hope-Johnson and Florence Eccles, were directors and principal shareholders but two men effectively managed the business. They were Thomas Coffey (chief distiller) and Joseph Cooney (company secretary). They also were minor shareholders. There was a shortage of whiskey in Britain, the stock at Locke's was, therefore, valuable. It could fetch at least £650,000 in the right places overseas.

A Mrs Chappelle visited the distillery. She claimed to be representing a group called Trans-World Trust, which wished to purchase whiskey. The distillery did not sell any to her, but its directors put the business on the market. In April 1947, the company advertised the sale in distilling trade journals. Joseph Cooney and an associate, Peter McEvoy, made one of eight bids that were subsequently turned down. The company decided to seek fresh tenders in September.

On 15 April, officers of the Departments of Finance, Industry and Commerce and the Revenue Commissioners met representatives of Irish distilling firms. At that meeting, Mr Cooney, representing Locke's, mentioned that his company might be changing hands. He therefore recommended some tightening up on the matter of licences for the sale of new fillings abroad and for export of mature spirits. On 21 May, Locke's solicitor, Edmund Mooney, responded to an invitation to meet the deputy secretary of the Department of Industry and Commerce, Denis Shanagher. Mr Shanagher pointed out the Minister's (Seán Lemass, Fianna Fáil) powers towards ensuring proper conduct of business. Mooney assured him that he would see that any purchaser of Locke's would acquaint the Department on future conduct of their distilling operations.

On 16 July, Cooney wrote to the Minister warning of the danger of the whiskey stocks in Locke's getting into 'speculative hands'. He also mentioned his own intention of joining with some friends to buy the business. The envelope was addressed to Lemass but the letter was sealed in another envelope inside. This bore Shanagher's name and appointment. Cooney and his associate, Peter McEvoy, met Shanagher on 23 July. The minutes of the meeting showed no request for an increase in the export quota for mature whiskey. They revealed that Cooney and McEvoy 'were concerned to see that, in the case of any change of ownership, the home market should not be adversely affected by any departure from the existing course of trading'.

A Clonmel solicitor, Thomas Morris, had a keen interest in coursing. He was discussing the possibility of introducing the sport to Switzerland with a Swiss national called Eindiguer. He mentioned that Locke's was for sale and Eindiguer organised a syndicate to buy the distillery. One main partner was Horace Smith, his English interpreter and assistant. Another minor player was German, Herr Saschsell. They represented the syndicate called Trans-World Trust of Lausanne, the one that Mrs Chappelle claimed to represent earlier that year. On 5 September 1947 the Trust engaged the auctioneering firm of Stokes and Quirke to negotiate the purchase on a 2% commission. Peter Quirke was a Fianna Fáil member of An Seanad. On 8 September, he accompanied Eindiguer, Smith and Morris to Kilbeggan. They questioned the export quota, but expressed general satisfaction at what was on offer and the Trust authorised Stokes and Quirke to offer £305,000 for Locke's Distillery.

On the morning on which tenders were to be opened, 9 September 1947, Quirke and Cooney visited the Department and spoke to two assistant principal officers, Messrs Murray and O'Neill. There is no record of what took place, but later in the day, Quirke met Mooney and arranged for a delay in opening tenders until 4.30 p.m. When that took place, the bid from the Trans-World Trust of Lausanne was successful. The parties concerned drafted contracts showing Eindiguer as the sole purchaser.

For a government department, things were moving quickly, because, in the same afternoon, a Ministerial conference with an agenda of 22 items approved an increase in Locke's export quota. Interestingly, Cork Distillery Company also got an increase that had been refused earlier in the year.

For the moment, everybody seemed to be satisfied with the Locke's deal. (There were allegations later of Quirke advising Eindiguer to present An Taoiseach, Eamonn de Valera [Fianna Fáil], with a gold watch for himself and another for his son. See excerpt from Dáil Report below). The buyers signed the contract, but did not pay the deposit of £75,000 within 48 hours, as agreed. The time was extended but still no payment was forthcoming. The auctioneers became worried and as weeks passed they began to doubt the Trust's integrity. They repudiated the contract of sale and conveyed their concern to the Garda Síochána and to the Department of Justice.

On 29 September, Gardaí found Eindiguer at a hotel in Dun Laoghaire and examined his passport. It seemed to be in order. They asked a few questions, but did not apprehend him.

The Gardai failed to find Smith until 1 October, when they interviewed him in Hatch Street Dublin. By then, they had ascertained that he had used a passport obtained under false pretences to enter the country. They discovered that his real name was Alexander Maximoe. He was wanted by the British police. Gardaí took Smith into custody and, the following day, having obtained a deportation order from the Minister for Justice, put him on the Holyhead boat with two policemen as an escort. When the policemen relaxed and Maximoe disappeared from the vessel, everybody assumed that he had jumped ship and was drowned. Some sources suggest, however, that he arranged a pick-up craft and got back to England, safe and well. He may even have been joined there by Eindiguer, who moved out of his hotel on 1 October, left the country and was never seen again. Herr Saschell abandoned a farm and residence he had bought at Ballygeagin House, near Gort, Co. Galway and went abroad. Some say he was instructed by the authorities to do so for his own good. The eventual tribunal stated that 'he was the subject of several confidential police reports', and that 'in the month of June 1947, he was informed that he would not be permitted to reside in this country after the end of that month'. It did not say who so informed him.

President Seán T. O'Kelly and Mrs O'Kelly entertained Saschsell, Eindiguer, Maximoe, a Mr Seamus Sweeney and Mrs Maire Sweeney at Aras an Uachtarán.

Meanwhile a vigorous, outspoken Teachta Dáil from the Laois-Offaly constituency, Oliver J. Flanagan (then a Monetary Reform deputy), was alleging political patronage in the deal. At Question Time in the House on 22 October, the matter came up:

Captain Giles (Meath-Westmeath, Fine Gael) asked the Minister for Industry and Commerce if his attention has been drawn to the proposed sale of Locke's Distillery, Kilbeggan, County Westmeath: whether he will state if this important industrial concern will continue to function under its proposed new owners; and if it will be subject to the operation of the Control of Manufactures Acts; and if so, whether this change in ownership has come officially before him, under the provisions of these Acts.

Mr Flanagan asked the Minister for Industry and Commerce whether his Department had been made aware of the transfer of Locke's Distillery, Kilbeggan, County Westmeath, to a Swiss syndicate; whether he has any information at his disposal concerning the future of this industry, and if any proposals have been laid before his Department in this connection; and if he will make a statement regarding whether or not the terms of the Control of Manufactures Acts are being complied with in connection with this transaction.

Mr Lemass: I propose to take questions Nos. 7 and 8 together. My attention has been drawn to the proposed sale of Locke's Distillery, Kilbeggan. I am not aware whether the sale has been completed, nor have I any information regarding the future of this industry. The Control of Manufactures Acts would not apply in the event of the distillery being sold, so that the question of compliance with the requirements of those Acts does not arise.

Mr Flanagan: Arising out of the Minister's reply, I would like to know if the Minister has any information of representations being made to his Department concerning the question of obtaining an export licence for 66,000 gallons of whiskey from the distillery.

Mr Lemass: No such application has been made and I may say that if such an application were made the licence would not be granted.

Mr Flanagan: Can the Minister say if a member of the Oireachtas made any verbal representations to his Department, and if so, what was the nature of the undertaking given to that member of the Oireachtas primarily concerned in the sale?

Mr Lemass: No such representations were made and no undertaking was given.

Mr Flanagan: Is it not a fact that the Department of Industry and Commerce was bitterly opposed to this sale falling into the hands of aliens and what is the reason for the fact that they changed [their minds]?

Mr Lemass: The solicitor of the company informed the Department of Industry and Commerce that the distillery was for sale. The Department has no power to prevent the sale even to persons of alien nationality because it is exempted from the provisions of the Control of Manufactures Act, as were all industries which were in existence before the Act was passed. I made known my view that the sale should be confined to firms that proposed to carry on the business in a proper way. The solicitor undertook to inform the Department if any offer so made was accepted but, in fact, no information has come from the solicitor since ...

Mr Dillon (Cavan-Monaghan, Independent): There seems to be a very unsavoury atmosphere about this whole transaction.

Mr Lemass: There will be, if Deputy Dillon gets his hands on it.

The adjournment debate the same day went as follows:

An Leas-Cheann Comhairle: Deputy Flanagan gave notice today that he would raise on the adjournment the subject-matter of Question 23 on today's Order Paper. I want to point out that the Minister will be called upon at 10.30 and must get his full ten minutes to reply.

Minister for Justice (Mr Boland) [Roscommon, Fianna Fáil]: Or earlier.

Mr Flanagan: This country in recent years has experienced very many rackets. The country has experienced cheating by chancers of all sorts and sizes. When the Government's attention was drawn to a glaring case of injustice and corruption some few months ago against a member of the Government, the Taoiseach was good enough to order an inquiry to investigate very fully the circumstances of such allegations. The subject-matter of the question that I am about to raise tonight with the Minister for Justice equally demands inquiry as did the case of Dr Ward a few months ago [another controversy].

Today I asked the Minister for Justice, 'Whether he is aware if any Swiss nationals came to this country in connection with the sale of Locke's Distillery, Kilbeggan, County Westmeath; if so, if he will give their names, the dates of arrival and departure, and whether they came under police observation while in this country.'

The Minister replied saying, 'I do not think it desirable that any official records which may exist as regards the movements or business of persons who come to this country from abroad should be made public, unless in a particular case some public interest would be served by doing so. I must therefore decline to give the information asked for by the Deptuy.'

I think that is most extraordinary in a case where we have had ample proof of the activities of those people who came to this country for the purpose of purchasing one of Ireland's oldest established industries. The manner in which they conducted themselves certainly calls for attention. I may say that if inquiries were addressed to the Minister concerning people coming here from abroad for the purpose of an honest-to-God, straightforward deal, there would certainly be no obligation on the Minister to give information concerning the activities of those people; but when a member of this House or when the general public have information at their disposal that those people who came over here for the pur-pose of purchasing that distillery were international chancers of fame, I think it is most desirable that this House should be given an opportunity of hearing who those people were, hearing the dates on which they came to this country and of their activities while in the country, and the nature of the work they performed during their stay in the country to carry out the necessary business in connection with Locke's Distillery.

I asked the Minister if those people were under police observation. The Minister has refused point blank to give this House any idea whether those people were under police observation, despite the fact that there was another question to the Minister when he replied that they were under police observation and that one of those referred to in the question was arrested and deported.

The Minister is very well aware of the fact that negotiations were proceeding for the sale of this distillery to a firm in Switzerland. He is also aware of the fact that a group of Irish citizens made an attempt to take over and develop and to improve the conditions in this distillery, and that the Government refused to receive a deputation to discuss the matter and refused to entertain the claims of Irish nationals for this distillery, good, bad or indifferent, whilst on the other hand a group of foreigners, the international chancers that I have referred to, have come over here and have found a spot in the hearts of Fianna Fáil henchmen. Those are the very people who have been favoured in connection with Locke's Distillery. The Minister is aware of the fact that yesterday a communication arrived to the solicitor concerned with the sale to say that a nephew of the President of Ireland was to complete the sale through a Senator of the Fianna Fáil Party on behalf of those citizens in Switzerland. Surely, that is a state of affairs on which this House is entitled to some information. The House is entitled to call for an inquiry and an investigation into this whole matter.

I should be very glad if the Minister would explain to this House, in view of the allegations that have been made against the Minister for Industry and Commerce and against Senator Quirke and also against other prominent Government representatives, as well as this gentleman to whom I have referred, why he refuses to give the information that I have asked for in my Question. Is it because the Minister would feel embarrassed at giving the names and the addresses of the very people who were entertained in Aras an Uachtarán? What explanation can be given, or what must the opinion of all Irish citizens be, when the President or head of this State should entertain people of such a low standard as the type of chancers we have seen here in connection with this sale?

An Leas-Cheann Comhairle: How they were entertained does not arise even on your own Question.

Mr Flanagan: I am asking the Minister for Justice for information concerning those people. The Minister has refused to supply me with that information. I say that the reason the Minister has refused to supply the information is because the Minister is afraid that if he supplied the information ask-

85

ed for in my Question, we are going to have a second national scandal in this country.

An Leas-Cheann Comhairle: The Deputy did not put anything down in his Question as to how they were entertained. He asked if they were under police observation.

Mr Flanagan: I am not querying about their entertainment now, but I am defying the Minister to give me the information that I asked for in my Question today. The Minister has very good reasons for withholding the information, in order to safeguard the names of his colleagues and in order to safeguard a certain Minister of State that has a keen personal interest in the question of the sale of Locke's Distillery. The Minister is very well aware of the fact that the name of one of those gentlemen was Mr Eindiguer, and that this gentleman came over here in his own plane. The Minister knows the people, the persons who met this gentleman and his colleagues on this business of the question of the purchase of Locke's Distillery.

An Leas-Cheann Comhairle: Who met him does not arise.

Mr Flanagan: It does arise.

An Leas-Cheann Comhairle: Not out of your Question.

Mr Flanagan: Yes. I have asked the Minister for the dates of the arrival and departure of this gentleman. I have respectfully asked the Minister to give the information. I say that the Minister is deliberately withholding this information from the House and that he knows perfectly well the date that these gentlemen came,

and the date that they left, and that he has records at his disposal concerning their activities. I have certain information at my disposal which I am prepared to hand over to the Minister and which would have very serious consequences if an investigation or an inquiry is held, in so far as this gentleman, Mr Georges Eindiguer, stated in the presence of a number of citizens in a certain hotel in this city that it was suggested by Senator Quirke that it might be a nice friendly gesture if Mr Eindiguer would bring over a gold watch and give it to the Taoiseach's son as a present in order to soften things. That is a statement I can stand over; that is a statement that was made by Senator Quirke to Mr Eindiguer.

An Leas-Cheann Comhairle: The Deputy is making charges which do not arise in any way out of his Question.

Mr Flanagan: I am making charges which I can stand over and that is the reason I am inviting an inquiry.

An Leas-Cheann Comhairle: They are not in the Deputy's Question.

An Ceann Comhairle resumed the Chair.

Mr Flanagan: I believe we have an outstanding case that those Swiss citizens were here for no good purpose. I respectfully submit that I am in a position to convince the Minister that the mission that brought those Swiss citizens to this country was not a good one. It is my duty as a citizen and as a Deputy, as it is the duty of every citizen and every Deputy, if I know of cases where there is either smuggling or black marketing going on, to have that reported to the proper Minister so that the necessary action may be taken by the Minister. I have endeavoured to convey to the Minister that these gentlemen came over here for the purpose of black marketing whiskey. That was the purpose which brought them over. Sixty-six thousand gallons of whiskey from this distillery at Kilbeggan were to be sold by those irresponsible Swiss citizens at £11 per gallon in the black market to a Mr Jameson, representing Messrs James Stewart and Co., Distillers, Park Lane, London, and for this purchase in the black market they were to get £660,000.

An Ceann Comhairle: The Deputy has nothing about that in his Question. He asked for the names and the purpose for which they were here and the dates of arrival and departure of Swiss nationals.

Mr Flanagan: I asked also if these Swiss nationals were under police observation while in this country.

An Ceann Comhairle: Yes.

Mr Flanagan: The Minister failed to reply. I maintain that these people were under police observation in this country. I have good reason to believe that the Minister has ample

87

information about the dealings in black market whiskey these people were engaged in and that he has deliberately withheld it from this House for certain reasons.

An Ceann Comhairle: The Deputy might let the Minister in.

Mr Flanagan: I very much regret to have to occupy the time of the House. I am sorry to say that, through the failure of the Government, Locke's good old distillery at Kilbeggan has now fallen into the hands of these people. Word came yesterday from the solicitors that the sale is to go through on behalf of those aliens by a friend of the President, a Mr McSweeney, a well-known barrister in Dublin who, in my opinion, is equally as good a chancer as these other chancers.

An Ceann Comhairle: The Deputy is making a scandalous use of his privileges in this House by introducing the names of men who cannot defend themselves, quite apart from the Question he asked.

Mr Flanagan: It can be proved.

Mr Killilea [Galway North, Fianna Fáil]: He said more scandalous things than that before you came in.

Mr Cafferky [Mayo South, Clann na Talmhan]: It can be proved. If these statements are scandalous, is it not open to the Government to establish an inquiry into the conduct of these gentlemen?

An Ceann Comhairle: It is not open to a Deputy to make a whole lot of charges which there is no opportunity of answering by the people concerned.

Mr Flanagan: Set up an inquiry.

Dr O'Higgins [Laois-Offaly, Fine Gael]: Before the Minister replies, I should like, in the public interest and in the interest of the good name of this country, to advise and warn the Government that very great damage may be done to the reputation of this country if there is any such thing as failure to give full information or any attempt to closure some of the references made here. Some of the references may appear entirely unwarranted, but I want the Minister to take this from me – that the statements made here tonight are comparatively tiny compared with some of the statements that are rolling round this country at the moment with regard to the manipulations and acrobatics and all the rest in connection with the proposed sale of Locke's Distillery to certain continentals. There does appear to be at least this much fire behind the smoke, and that is how the fire is being fanned, namely, that these particular premises were on the market and there was no great encouragement given in the direction of facilitating the sale to any outsider; in fact there was discouragement. Then a particular group of foreigners under rather big political patronage arrived in the country and within 24 hours of their arrival –

Mr Boland: We know how it is being fanned now.

Dr O'Higgins: The Minister can take some people as being sincere other than himself.

Mr Boland: I pick those whom I consider to be sincere.

Dr O'Higgins: We will leave the Minister to his corrupt selection. Meanwhile he will get the truth from me. The Minister knows when to interrupt. Within 24 hours of their arrival they were able to enter a Minister's office and get documents and evidence of trade facilities. Later on those were challenged or withdrawn or threatened to be withdrawn. In the meantime, there was a falling out between the negotiators. It seems extraordinary that foreigners, or any group of financiers from abroad, should get such an immediate entry and that subsequently one of them was found worthy of deportation. There is an amount to be inquired into and it will do harm to close down on this.

Mr Cafferky: Will the Minister state –

Mr Boland: I am entitled to reply.

An Ceann Comhairle: The Minister is entitled to reply.

Mr Boland: I am prepared to sit here as long as Deputies are allowed to speak.

An Ceann Comhairle: The Minister to reply.

Mr Cafferky: May I ask a question?

An Ceann Comhairle: No. The Minister has ten minutes to reply.

Mr Boland: I never heard that there was a charge made against the Minister for Industry and Commerce until I heard Deputy Flanagan say so tonight. It is the first I heard of it or of a charge against Senator Quirke. I was asked if I was aware that Swiss nationals came to this country in connection with the sale of Locke's Distillery; if I would give their names and the dates of arrival and departure; and whether they came under police observation while in this country. In reply I stated:

> I do not think it desirable that any official records which may exist as regards the movement or business of persons who come to this country from abroad should be made public, unless in a particular case some public interest would be served by doing so. I must therefore decline to give the information asked for by the Deputy.

Of course, when supplementary questions were raised it was immediately clear to me that there was a public interest to be served and I asked the Ceann Comhairle to make sure that this question would be allowed to be raised. I propose to give the history of this matter so far as I know it. A Mr Georges Eindigeur arrived at Shannon airport on 3 September, not in his own plane as the Deputy stated, but in an ordinary plane. He informed the immigration officer that he was coming on a business visit to a well-known south of Ireland business. I do not like to use the name of any outsider, but this is a very well-known businessman who is not a supporter of the Government, quite the reverse.

Mr McGrath [Cork City, Fianna Fáil]: He is a well-known Fine Gael supporter in Clonmel.

Mr Boland: He is not a supporter of ours.

Mr Donnellan [Galway North, Clann na Talmhan]: Some people know who he is.

Mr Boland: He was accompanied by Alexander Maximoe, who was then posing as Horace Henry Smith and who held a British passport. I am reading this so that I may be accurate. Information reached the Department of Justice towards the end of September that Mr Eindiguer had entered into a contract to purchase Locke's. At the same time it was discovered that Messrs Eindiguer and Maximoe were associating with an alien who had orders to leave the country. The police were then instructed by my Department to make inquiries regarding Messrs Eindiguer and Maximoe. In a few days Maximoe's real identity was discovered and an order for his deportation was issued at once by me. I should mention that there is no evidence of any fraudulent activity on the part of Mr Eindiguer. I understand that in the negotiations to purchase the distillery he was represented by a well-known Dublin firm of solicitors, and that a well-known firm of auctioneers acted as his agents.

Mr Flanagan: A very well-known auctioneer – Senator Quirke.

Mr Boland: Very well-known auctioneers – Messrs Stokes and Quirke. His credentials, as they appeared to those firms, might be summed up in the words used by *The Irish Times*, on 6 October, namely:

> Mr Eindiguer is a well-known figure in international trade and has completed big deals on behalf of industrialists in Switzerland, South America and other countries. He visited Ireland on behalf of important interests to investigate the possibilities of increased whiskey exports to South America, where there is a considerable market for the product. Exporters last night said that the trade, apart from the purchase price, would help to create important dollar credits abroad.

... I understand that, in fact, the deal has not been completed and that published statements that the purchase price has been paid are not correct. It was stated in *The Irish Times* that the deal was completed.

Mr Flanagan: In the *Irish Press*.

Mr Boland: I got a telephone message to my own house from a friend of mine who told me that he wanted to communicate a very important matter to me. I told this friend to come along. When I got his information, I immediately rang up an official of the Aliens Section of my Department and told him to bring along the chief superintendent in charge of the Special Branch of the Garda Síochána. They came to me almost immediately – within an hour. The outcome of that was that this man who had been passing as Smith was identified as Maximoe. He was arrested in a flat in Dublin occupied by another alien. I had not followed the details and I said that I thought he was arrested at the Aer Lingus offices.

The police knew that he was to leave by air but he never turned up. They were watching his luggage. I then signed a deportation order. The guards went out to this house and got him there.

Mr Flanagan: The house of a friend of the Minister.

Mr Boland: Not at all.

Mr Flanagan: I shall give his name.

Mr Boland: I do not care what his name is, he is no friend of mine.

An Ceann Comhairle: Order!

Mr Flanagan: He is an alien who sold £25,000 worth of Irish tweed to get dollars for you.

Mr Boland: He is no friend of mine. I do not know who the man is but he is under notice to quit this country.

Mr Flanagan: He got the dollars for you.

Mr Boland: He is not naturalised. He is under orders to leave the country but he was allowed time to complete his business.

Mr Cafferky: Is it true that Scotland Yard came over for him?

Mr Boland: They were after Maximoe.

Mr Cafferky: We have the whole story.

Mr Boland: With regard to the questions addressed to me this afternoon, I have a little note here. As the Minister for Industry and Commerce said this afternoon, no application was made for an export licence for 60,000 gallons of matured whiskey.

Mr Flanagan: Senator Quirke was at the office.

Mr Boland: There was no application made and if it had been made, it would have been refused. Locke's have a normal export permit for 4,000 gallons per annum and this doubled as it had been the practice to do for all such small distilleries who made application. The total quantity allowed to be exported from the whole country is 500,000 gallons per annum. If an application had been made for the export of 60,000 gallons or any other similarly large quantity of whiskey by this firm, it would have been refused. It was put up to the Department that the 4,000 gallons should be increased and it was increased to 8,000 gallons per year. These

92

people, however, were told that unless this distillery was kept as a going concern or if any attempt was made to dissipate their stocks, any export licences granted would be withdrawn. In regard to the visit to the President, unfortunately that did happen. It is very difficult to check everyone who comes forward. People actually get to see the heads of State in other countries who are not all that is desirable. It did happen that this group did go to the President and it was as a result of the publication of that and the fact that one particular name appeared, that this man who came to me got suspicious of the whole crowd. It was published in the papers in the morning of the day on which this friend of mine came to me to tell me of his suspicions. The result is that one has been shifted out. The other man was all the time under notice. We have curtailed the notice as a result of his action in this transaction.

Mr Cafferky: How long was Scotland Yard over here before they intercepted this man?

EVENTUALLY, DÁIL ÉIREANN passed a resolution on November 6 1947 and next day the Taoiseach, Eamon de Valera ordered a judicial inquiry under a tribunal of High Court Judges to investigate Deputy Flanagan's allegations. The Tribunal (Cahir Davitt, Kevin Haugh and John O'Byrne) held eighteen sittings between 14 November and 11 December. Forty-nine people gave evidence on oath. Most of these bore prominent names. Included was the Taoiseach and Minister for External Affairs, Eamon De Valera. Others were Seán Lemass, T.D., Tánaiste and Minister for Industry and Commerce and Supplies; James Dillon T.D.; General Richard Mulcahy and Dr Tom O'Higgins T.D. Oliver Flanagan gave evidence too. An assistant principal officer at the Department of Finance, Peter Berry, gave evidence. He was to be a prominent witness in a much later case that became known as 'The Arms Trial'. Patrick McGilligan (Dublin North-West, Fine Gael) declined an invitation to give evidence.

The report of the tribunal recorded much of the afore-going. In the main, it found them to be without foundation and it was critical of Flanagan.

Flanagan called Locke's secretary, Joseph Cooney, and his son, also Joseph. Their evidence clashed with his own. The younger John Cooney stated that Flanagan took notes at a meeting he had with him. Flanagan, who had denied this, was called in and Cooney repeated the allegation. Flanagan did not cross-examine. Desperate, he called for Eindiguer, Saschell and two foreign ladies, hitherto unmentioned, to be summoned as witnesses. The Tribunal refused, alleging triviality on the part of the Deputy. Its final report, issued in December 1947, questioned Oliver Flanagan's integrity, saying that his evidence continued to shift regarding some Minister having a personal interest in the sale of the distillery. The Tribunal stated:

> There is not a scintilla of evidence that any minister had a particle of such interest. The charge is an extremely grave one. We are satisfied that it is wholly untrue, that it is entirely without foundation and was made with a degree of reckless-ness amounting to complete irresponsibility.

The Tribunal found Flanagan to be 'uncandid'. He appeared to be directing replies to questions 'elsewhere than to the Tribunal'. He contradicted himself, and shifted ground 'when he found that answers given would lead him where he did not wish to go'.

Flanagan was held up to ridicule, but he had the last laugh. Proving that rural Ireland always believes that there is 'no smoke without fire', voters in Laois-Offaly increased Flanagan's poll-topping total by 5,000 to 14,370. It was February 1948. Pantomime stars were pounding out parodies. They contained references to gold Swiss watches and 'Locke's of Flanagan's hair'. Like this, to the air of MacNamara's Band:

> My name is Oliver Flanagan, I'm a divil in the Dáil,
> Especially when it comes to making dirt of Fianna Fáil.
> Their Christmas jar was whiskey – from Kilbeggan, they don't drink Scotch –

As much as they want for nothing, save a wink and an old
Swiss watch.

POSTSCRIPT

Fianna Fáil lost eight seats in the election that followed (18
February 1948) and lost power for the first time since 1932. A
new Inter-Party government was formed. Locke's took the
distillery off the market and tried again to re-energise the
business.

At Question Time in the Dáil on 6 December 1950, Mr
John Tully (Cavan-Monaghan, Clann na Poblachta) asked the
Minister for Industry and Commerce if, in view of the fact
that a sufficiently great quantity of whiskey was not being
exported by Irish distillers, he would set up a distillery
whose product would be for export only. Mr Cosgrave, Parliamentary Secretary to the Minister answered, 'The setting up
of a whiskey distillery is primarily a matter for private
enterprise, and without special legislation, I would have no
power to enter this industry'.

Further improvements could not save Locke's and distilling ended there in 1953. A receiver moved in on 26
November 1958. He sold off a portion of the stock of mature
whiskey. Later Karl Heinz Mellor purchased the residue of
stock and the premises for £10,000. After being used for
miscellaneous purposes including the housing of pigs and
parts for cars, the Kilbeggan community moved in and, with
the assistance of a FÁS scheme, restored part of Locke's
Distillery. Today, conducted tours of the old distilling area
take place and there is a museum, craft shop and restaurant.
Cooley Distillers use another section as a bonded warehouse.
On 17 July 1992 Locke's Pure Pot Still single malt Irish
whiskey appeared again on the market. It is distilled in
Cooley, Co. Louth and matures in Kilbeggan. Often, when a
glass or two of the golden amber is drunk, tales are told
about the 'Locke's Distillery Scandal' of 1947 because
whenever *uisce beatha* is drunk, reports from Government

Inquiries are ignored; what lies between lines is magnified
and, sure as God, a scandal still emerges.

THE BATTLE OF BALTINGLASS

Oh, the G.P.O. in Dublin will go down in history:
'Twas there the glorious fight was made that set our country
  free:
But from Aughrim down to Bolands Mill there's nothing could
  surpass,
The siege of the Sub-Post Office in the Town of Baltinglass.

There were Bren-guns and Sten-guns and whippet tanks
  galore,
The battle raging up and down from pub to general store:
Between the vintner and the cook the pot was quite upset,
And the Minister swore this Irish stew was the worst he ever
  'et.

County Wicklow was the last stronghold of the 1798 Rebellion. Around the Glen of Imaal, Michael Dwyer and a few followers held out for some years until Robert Emmet's abortive rising in 1803 precipitated a major drive to root them out. The spirit of Wicklow protesters proved no less enthusiastic in the twentieth-century 'Battle of Baltinglass'. Here a nation's freedom was not the driving force. Impetus stemmed from loyalty, a perceived sense of fair play and justice. This was no peasant rising. Protestant landlords sided with humble villagers and astounded them by insisting on playing their part in whatever hardships were necessary to insist on right, as they assessed it, being done. Nobody fired a shot in this conflict but the campaign was run almost on military lines, demonstrating a knowledge of the power of public opinion that was before its time.

A family named Cooke had conducted the business of Baltinglass Post Office since 1870. Michael Cooke was the first to do so and one of his large family joined His Majesty's Excise Service. Stationed in Scotland, he married a local girl and they had a daughter, Helen. The family moved back to Ireland and during the War of Independence, Helen carried out Cumann na mBan duties. For a time too, she assisted in the publication of the underground news-sheet, the *Irish Bulletin*. In 1935, she took up an appointment as sub-postmistress in Rathdrum, Co. Wicklow, about 20 miles from her father's home in Baltinglass, where her Aunt Brigid was sub-postmistress. The following year Brigid became ill. Her sisters, Mary and Kate, knew little about the Post Office, so Helen came to Baltinglass to help. Within a short time Brigid and Mary died. Kate sought the appointment of sub-postmistress. She was well over the age-limit, so the Naas postmaster offered the post to Helen instead. She refused, saying it was her aunt's right, and Kate got the job. It was Helen, of course, who ran the Post Office. She also attended to her aunt, especially a decade later when Kate suffered a number of strokes. The worst of these, in 1950, left Kate severely handicapped and, assuming that Helen would replace her officially, she resigned from the appointment of sub-postmistress. Helen applied for it.

Weeks passed and Helen became anxious when she received no notification from her district postmaster in Naas. She confided in her parish priest, Fr Doyle. He got a number of prominent people in Baltinglass to countersign his own recommendation to the National Labour Party Minister for Post and Telegraphs, Mr James Everett, that Helen be appointed. Mr Everett was a Wicklow deputy. Bernie Sheridan, formerly from Ballinalee, Co. Longford, promised to contact his friend, General Sean MacEoin (Longford-Westmeath, Fine Gael), the Minister for Justice, if Helen Cooke did not get the expected call.

Someone else was awaiting news about the Post Office. Michael Farrell, son of a draper and publican, a lieutenant in the FCA (Forsa Cosanta Áitiúl, formerly the Local Defence Force) was also an applicant. Because of his lack of experience in Post Office duties, Miss Cooke discounted him as a serious contender. Many more weeks passed until, one October afternoon, she learned that Farrell had been appointed.

Villagers voiced their support for Helen and registered protests in a number of ways. They crossed political divides. Prominent Baltinglass men Paul Keogh, Godfrey Timmons and Paddy O'Grady accompanied Bernie Sheridan when, true to his word, he travelled to meet Seán MacEoin in Leinster House about the matter.

He also sought press coverage from the *Irish Press* but learned that, to get it, the protesters would have do something newsworthy. He thought about this a number of times over the next few days, because MacEoin had told him he should have come to him before the appointment of Farrell and that he could do nothing at such a late stage.

Independent Farmers' deputy Patrick Cogan of Tullow knew Baltinglass and Helen Cooke. When he questioned James Everett privately, the Minister told him that there had been complaints about the way Miss Cooke had run the Post Office. Cogan asked the Naas postmaster if he had heard any criticism. He had not.

Felix O'Neill, grocer, Ben Cooper, vocational teacher, and those already mentioned began organising a protest committee. The local curate, Fr Moran, sent Cooper to Oliver J. Flanagan, Independent T.D. in Mountmellick, Co. Laois. Flanagan could do nothing. Why? He had helped get the appointment for Farrell. His cousin had enlisted his aid and he had seen the Minister about it. However, he assured Ben that if he had come earlier, he might well have made as much of an effort on behalf of Miss Cooke!

An ad hoc planning group met on 25 November 1950 and decided to hold a formal public protest meeting in the Town Hall the following Monday. They discussed placards and public address equipment. On the same evening a deputation met Oliver Flanagan in his Mountmellick home. They pointed out the circumstances in which Helen Cooke found herself, looking after a near-invalid on nothing. They asked him to get her a vacant Employment Exchange position in Baltinglass. Flanagan promised to try. Nothing materialised.

There was considerable activity in Baltinglass and surrounding areas on 26 November. Villagers came out of doors when they heard a loud voice. Bernie Sheridan shouted 'Baltinglass Calling, Baltinglass Calling' from a public address loudspeaker mounted on his car. He followed this with an address. People still remembered the German propaganda broadcasts of 'Lord Haw-Haw' on the radio during World War II. This was always preceded by the signature phrase: 'Germany Calling, Germany Calling'. A few smiled but most of them took notice. Appointments on the committee still were not filled. Fr Moran declined the vital chairmanship, so the organisers decided to ask Major General Meade Dennis. This retired British army officer farmed and had a successful dairy herd at nearby Fortgranite. Chemist Des Cullen telephoned him and he promised to consider it. While so doing, he had a visit from Fr Moran. The priest reminded him that his great-grand-father had appointed the first Cooke to Baltinglass Post Office 80 years before. Immediately, Dennis became fired with a zeal for the cause of Miss Cooke. Because of Fr Moran's information, this no longer constituted meddling in a village quarrel; it amounted to a serious family responsibility. Of course he would accept chairmanship! The very model of a modern Major General went to review his troops in preparation for the 'Battle of Baltinglass'.

People were slow to arrive at the Town Hall on Monday evening – until Bernie Sheridan urged them with 'Baltinglass Calling' and reminded them that the meeting was about to start. Then they packed the building. Dennis delivered an explanatory address before introducing, in turn, Deputies Paddy Cogan (Wicklow, Independent Farmer) and Thomas Brennan (Wicklow, Fianna Fáil). The chairman of West Wicklow Fine Gael, The O'Mahoney, had fallen from a horse but Colonel Christopher Mitchell deputised for him. Paul Keogh received overwhelming support for his proposal to send messages of protest to the President, the Taoiseach (John A. Costello, Dublin South East, Fine Gael), and the leaders of all political parties.

In the Dáil on 29 November, Paddy Cogan gave notice that he would raise on the adjournment the question of the manner in which the appointment had been made. The Minister was indisposed, but he faced his adversary later, on 6 December (see below).

THE SLAB

The job of sub-postmaster or mistress, as might be
Is not exactly one that leads to wealth and luxury;
But Korea was a picnic and Tobruk was just a pup
To the row the day the linesmen came to take the cable up.

There were gremlins from the Kremlin, and little men from Mars
Complete with flying saucers and hats festooned with stars.
There were rocket-firing, jet-propelled, atomic flying boats,
And Commandos from the G.P.O. in their oul' tarpaulin coats.

Sylvester Gaffney, pen-name for the celebrated ballad
writer Leo Maguire, recalled 30 November, when P and T
linesmen arrived in Baltinglass, installed a switchboard in
Farrell's and began digging a trench for the cables. Word
spread like wild-fire. Supporters of Miss Cooke passed by
and dropped remarks about there being an unpleasant smell
in the street.

The linesmen made a dash to open up the cable trench,
They opened up the sewer instead, Lord save us! what a stench!
A gentleman in jodhpurs swore 'By Jove, they're using gas
The next will be an atom bomb on peaceful Baltinglass'.

Dennis arrived and proposed a picket to stop the linesmen
from disconnecting the line from its present switchboard in
Miss Cooke's. His warning that picket members should be
prepared for anything, even arrest, did not deter volunteers.
It jogged Bernie Sheridan's memory, however. This might
be just what that journalist in the *Irish Press* required.

Bernie telephoned and asked. It was. A reporter and a
photographer arrived the next day. People holding placards marched outside Cooke's. Bernie Sheridan accepted
volunteers for picket duty. Two linesmen approached. John
Doyle stood in the doorway, expecting them to try gaining
entry. Instead, they moved towards a concrete slab that
covered the cable connections. Patrick O'Grady stood resolutely on this and ignored their request to remove it. They
went back to their gaffer at Farrell's.

Now General Dennis and his wife arrived and Mrs
Dennis insisted on being next to occupy the slab. A P and T

101

engineer came up. She refused to move, saying it would take policemen to arrest and remove her. The engineer also retreated to telephone his headquarters for further instructions. It has been alleged that they in turn called the Department of Posts and Telegraphs. Obviously they received instructions to call off the campaign temporarily. An elderly, delicate Madam O'Mahoney arrived to relieve Mrs Dennis 'on the slab'. Someone got a cane chair for her and brought her tea. Wrapped in a rug, because a cold winter sleet was spitting, she sipped it and presented a pathetic sight. The engineer, gaffer and linesmen left Baltinglass. They would return, but in the meantime the *Irish Press* had a front page story, with pictures, that would bring other newsmen flocking to witness the next offensive in the 'Battle of Baltinglass'.

A large front-page photograph showed Madam O'Mahoney on her 'slab throne' with Mrs Dennis and Bernie Sheridan beside a large poster outside the Post Office. It asked the question: 'Are these the human rights Mr Everett spoke about at Strasbourg?' Another picture showed Miss Cooke serving some contented-looking customers.

Because of the sympathy evoked by the apparent injustice to a middle-aged spinster who was looking after her invalid aunt, Michael Farrell's side of the Baltinglass story was ignored almost completely. He had given good service in two voluntary Defence Forces of his country. Young and fit, he had plenty to offer in the job. He had applied for it and people knew that. Most important from his point of view, he had been appointed. The danger of losing it through interference of neighbours was distressful. Michael Farrell had supporters too. They awaited their own chance to make their presence felt.

The protest committee visited *The Irish Times* and its editor, Bertie Smyllie, promised support. The committee then set up an intelligence service that succeeded in finding out Post Office engineers' plans in advance. During off-duty hours, they withdrew pickets but Bernie Sheridan installed a warning siren that would recall them to duty if the need arose. When her superiors instructed Helen Cooke to continue running the Post Office, there was some joy but considerable apprehension. During the first week of December, as newsmen and photographers booked every available bed in the town, an excited committee considered all sorts of projects. Picketing the Dáil, dropping leaflets on Dublin from an aeroplane, building a wall or barbed wire entanglement around 'the slab'. If one idea proved unfeasible, another emerged.

Villagers did attend the Dáil public gallery during a lively adjournment debate on 6 December. Paddy Cogan made a spirited defence of Miss Cooke and her 14 years of service. Cogan pointed out that the new location for the Post Office was 'a public house ... the headquarters of the Minister's party in Wicklow', and that the sub-postmaster designate was, 'the son of a county councillor of the Minister's party'.

'It is a quibble, a contemptible quibble, to suggest ... that [Miss Cooke] was not a direct employee of the Department,' he said, adding: 'There are complaints against every public official in this country from the highest to the lowest, but have there been any charges proved against Miss Cooke? ... I asked the postmaster of Naas if there had been any charges or irregularities of any kind proved against Miss Cooke, or even seriously alleged, and he told me that the sub-office in Baltinglass was one of the most regularly run, one of the most correctly run Post Offices in the country, and that if anything the two Miss Cookes, Miss Helen Cooke and her aunt, erred perhaps in being too strict in enforcing all the regulations of the Department of Posts and Telegraphs. Yet, this is the conscientious and faithful family that has been victimised.

'We have in Baltinglass this family of Miss Cooke and her aunt. They have run this Post Office for years. It is being taken from them now. Miss Helen Cooke's aunt is now an invalid. She is 83 years of age, she is in very feeble health and she is depending on her niece for her living. Yet these two poor defenceless people have been ruthlessly deprived of their sole means of livelihood in order to provide an appointment for a hanger-on of the Minister's political

Party ... I do not ask for tears from anybody. The people of Baltinglass do not want any tears shed. They are prepared to fight their battle through to the end, regardless of what opposition may be piled up against them.' J.P. Brennan, the Dun Laoghaire-Rathdown Clann na Poblachta deputy, reiterated Cogan's words. Then Cogan spoke of Helen Cooke's nationalist and Red Cross background. Admitting the merit of Farrell's LDF service, he added:

> There were hundreds of young men in the Baltinglass district who also served faithfully in the LDF but they did not seek to take from Miss Cooke her means of livelihood. The only merit that the successful applicant can claim is that he is the son of a man who was a member of the county council up to the last election, and who is a member of the Minister's Party.
> The issue ... is whether we are to have public positions filled on the basis of merit alone or on the basis of political graft and corruption. That is the clear-cut issue raised by the people of Baltinglass upon which they are prepared to stand vigorously to the end. There is no merit whatever on the side of this appointment. It bears on its face all the marks of the cold-blooded brutality and immorality of Soviet rule. The Minister has many times denounced in Wicklow Red rule and Communism. He has even accused members of the Labour Party of Communism. What is Communism but a form of gangsterism which fills up appointments, not on merit, but on the basis of those who served most faithfully on the Party line?[The people of Baltinglass] have lighted a fire which has spread throughout the land. It is a fire which will blaze and burn until the public life of this country is finally and permanently cleansed.

Towards the end of his long speech, there were interruptions from Jack McQuillan (Roscommon, Independent), John O'Leary (Waterford, National Labour), Michael Moran (Mayo South, Fianna Fáil), Oliver Flanagan, and the Minister for Posts and Telegraphs in the previous (1944-48) government, Paddy Little (Waterford, Fianna Fáil).

The Minister responded:

> The difficulties which have arisen in filling the sub-postmastership of Baltinglass arise from a decision of mine in 1948. Some time after I became Minister for Posts and Telegraphs I instructed my Department that in future sub-offices should not be transferred to relatives except when the applicant was a husband, wife, son, daughter, brother, sister, widower or widow of the outgoing sub-postmaster.

Amid calls to 'Shut up', from McQuillan, Paddy Smith (Cavan-Monaghan, Fianna Fáil) accused the Minister of lying and would not withdraw the statement when the Leas Cheann Comhairle (Patrick Hogan, Clare, Labour) so instructed. Then he called Mr Everett a 'low down rat'.

'If I go over there' – threatened Oliver Flanagan (Newspaper reports suggest that the Minister for Lands, Joseph Blowick [Mayo, Clann na Talmhan], restrained him).

Mr Smith said the Leas Cheann Comhairle was partisan and 'a political hack'.

'You cannot name me because the Chair has to be occupied by the Ceann Comhairle and you are not Ceann Comhairle yet,' he shouted.

Peadar Cowan (Dublin North-East, Clann na Poblachta) called for a vote on the naming of Smith. Paddy Little asked if a vote could be taken after half-past-ten.

While all this was going on, the Baltinglass deputation in the public gallery found it difficult to restrain themselves. Bernie Sheridan passed some uncomplimentary remarks about the Minister. Mr Everett's wife was sitting near him and asked for his removal, but a Baltinglass garda happened to be on duty and he advised against it. Des Cullen was not so lucky. Although a friend of James Everett's, he jumped up and rebuked the Minister loudly. Guards ejected him.

The record of the debate ends: 'Grave disorder ensuing, the Leas Cheann Comhairle ... adjourned the Dáil at 10.55 p.m. until 10.30 a.m. the following morning, Thursday, 7 December 1950.

Next morning, the Taoiseach moved that Deputy Smith be suspended from service of the House. 'I beg to second that proposition,' Smith himself said. The proposition was carried by 65 votes to 47. Seán Lemass (Dublin South-Central, Fianna Fáil) asked the Ceann Comhairle (Frank Fahy, Galway South, Fianna Fáil) if others were to be named, saying 'there seems to me to have been a completely partisan administration by the Chair last night'. There was further disturbance during an amusing example of parliamentary behaviour when Deputy Smith withdrew from the chamber, but not from the precincts:

Mr Lemass: May I inquire if the Leas-Cheann Comhairle has any other report to make to the Chair?

An Ceann Comhairle: I have got no other report.

Mr Lemass: May I point out that, according to reports in the Press, there was considerable disorder in the Dáil last night and apparently the Leas-Cheann Comhairle is only taking notice of disorder on one side of the House?

An Cheann Comhairle: If the Leas-Cheann Comhairle is to be impeached, it must be done by a motion.

Mr Lemass: We will consider that, because there seems to me to have been a completely partisan administration by the Chair last night.

An Ceann Comhairle: I cannot listen to any more remarks on the Leas-Cheann Comhairle.

Mr Lemass: Did the Leas-Cheann Comhairle report to you that Deputies left their seats on the other side and crossed the floor of the House?

Mr C. Lehane [Dublin South Central, Clann na Poblachta]: That is not correct.

Mr Lemass: The Ceann Comhairle should inquire from the Leas-Cheann Comhairle on the matter.

An Ceann Comhairle: It is not my duty to do so. The Minister was refused a hearing last night.

Mr McGrath: So was Deputy Cogan.

Mr Lemass: The Minister was not the only person refused a hearing.

An Ceann Comhairle: The Chair might be given one now. The Minister was refused a hearing last night. The Minister is entitled to a hearing in this House.

Mr Lemass: So are Deputies; just as much entitled as the Minister.

An Ceann Comhairle: The Chair is entitled to a hearing and is not going to get it, apparently. The Minister is entitled to a hearing and the Minister did not get it. I propose that he gets ten minutes now.

Mr Lemass: He will not get it, as far as we are concerned.

Mr Smith (from the Lobby): The Minister lied last night. What about that?

A Deputy: Are you there still?

Mr Brennan: May I point out, a Chinn Chomhairle, that I was interested in some of the questions dealing with this matter? Due to the attitude of some of the members on the Government Benches last night when Deputy Cogan was speaking, they could not finish –

Minister for External Affairs (Mr MacBride) [Dublin South-West, Clann na Poblachta]: On a point of order –

Mr Smith (from the Lobby): Listen to Pontius Pilate.

Mr Brennan: He could not finish in time to allow me any time. May I press for time also to express my views clearly?

An Ceann Comhairle: Deputy Smith should leave the precincts of the House. By a vote of the House, his services have been dispensed with.

A Deputy: Go on, Pat.

A Deputy: He does not want to go now.

Mr Smith (from the Lobby): I am out of the House.

Minister for External Affairs (Mr MacBride): On a point of order –

An Ceann Comhairle: Deputy Smith must leave the precincts of the House.

Mr McQuillan: Go on out.

Mr Smith (from the Lobby): You put me out.

An Ceann Comhairle: Deputy Smith has not left the precincts of the House.

Mr McQuillan: Call the Sergeant-at-Arms.

Mr G. Boland: I think the Chair knows its own business and needs no prompting.

An Ceann Comhairle: The Chair has stated that Deputy Smith must leave the precincts of the House. That is clear. He has not done so. I adjourn the House for a quarter of an hour, to give Deputy Smith a chance of obeying the ruling of the House.

THE DÁIL ADJOURNED at 10.55 a.m. and resumed at 11.10 a.m.

Interestingly, at Question Time the same day, Gerald Bartley, the West Galway Fianna Fáil deputy, asked, 'was an applicant for an appointment as sub-postmistress at Kilmurvey, Aran, who had long experience in charge of a sub-office and in support of whose application the people of Kilmurvey petitioned his Department; and further, whether the Post Office has now been located in a licensed premises'.

Minister for Posts and Telegraphs (Mr Everett): One of the unsuccessful applicants for the position ... was employed during the years 1935-1941 as an assistant at a sub-Post Office by her mother who was the sub-postmistress. A memorial from a number of local residents was received on behalf of that applicant. The sub-Post Office at Kilmurvey is not located in a licensed premises.

Bartley pointed out that the appointee's husband was a licensed hotel proprietor. The Kilmurvey case bore some similarities to Baltinglass, which again arose a short while later in the same Question Time.

An Ceann Comhairle: With reference to the excitement that arose in the debate last night in connection with the Baltinglass Post Office appointment, a compromise solution, let us say, has been reached by permission of the House. Deputy Lemass will speak for five minutes and the Minister will have ten minutes in which to reply.
Mr Corry: What is the position with regard to the notice which I gave to raise the subject matters of Questions 87, 88 and 89 on the Adjournment?
An Ceann Comhairle: That will be at five o'clock.
Mr Lemass: Before the Minister speaks on this Baltinglass affair, I think it is desirable to remind him and the House of the nature of the charge which been made against him. In April last the postmistress of Baltinglass, Miss K. Cooke, resigned. She was an old lady whose health did not permit of her continuing the work of the office – the work having, in fact, been done for the previous 14 years by her niece,

108

Miss Helen Cooke, and done by her to the general public's satisfaction. I understand that, in circumstances such as existed there, where a relative of the postmistress is available and qualified to carry on the work in the same premises, it has been the invariable practice of the Post Office not to advertise the vacancy, but to appoint the relative. In this particular case, however, the vacancy was advertised. It was assumed locally that the advertising of the vacancy was merely a formality and that inevitably Miss Helen Cooke would be appointed to the post. In consequence of that understanding, a number of people, who might otherwise have been candidates, either did not pursue their candidatures or withdrew them. Only one candidate sought the appointment in opposition to Miss Cooke, a Mr Michael Farrell. When it became known that there was opposition to the re-appointment of Miss Cooke from that quarter, representations were made in favour of her appointment by representatives of every class and section in the area. Miss Cooke had, in the opinion of the people using the Post Office, every qualification for the appointment. She was personally efficient and popular. She had 14 year's experience in the working of the office. She had available to her, premises which were in use as the Post Office in the area for some years and to which the telephone cables had recently been brought at considerable expense underground. She, as I said, had every possible qualification except one. She had no political pull.

The other candidate for the position was a Mr Michael Farrell, and he, so far as the views of the local inhabitants are concerned, had no qualifications for the office except one. He had political pull. This Mr Michael Farrell is the son of a prominent supporter of the Minister in his own constituency. He was a member of the Minister's Party on the Wicklow County Council. He was selected by the Minister's Party, the National Labour Party, to contest the Kildare seat in the last general election against the present Minister for Social Welfare. He failed to do so by reason of the fact that he was two minutes late with his nomination paper. He has, in the views of local people of all political opinions and all classes, no outstanding qualifications for the office. Let me say that in my view his political opinions and association with the Minister's Party is not necessarily a disqualification. The general view locally is that he is not a desirable person to be appointed. His father owns a public house. His father also owns a grocery business, a butchery business and a large drapery business in the town of Baltinglass.

A Deputy: More power to him.

Mr Lemass: There used to be a regulation in the Post Office which debarred the appointment to the position of postmaster or postmistress of any person who is concerned either directly or indirectly in the control or management of a licensed premises if other applicants had suitable premises available. I would be desirous of knowing from the Minister whether that regulation has also been amended or cancelled to permit of this appointment. The Minister has a choice between this person, whose father was a prominent and wealthy businessman in the town of Baltinglass, and who was without experience or qualification, as against a lady who has no other means of livelihood, who had 14 years' experience of the post and who was recommended by the great majority of the local interests which used the Post Office.

I want to remove, if I may, the rather mean insinuation which the Minister attempted to make yesterday that the lady, Miss Cooke or her family, were in some way associated with the Castle [British] tradition. The Minister tried to justify his appointment on that insinuation. It is not a matter which concerns this issue. Even if the lady was not of the political opinions or religion of the majority, she would still be entitled to the appointment under the practice of the Department. But, in fact, the family have been for a long time intimately associated with the nationalist movement. On the face of it this looks like a discreditable political job. It is not merely a charge against the Minister. The Minister may have made a mistake. He may have been subjected to political pressure to make this appointment, but having made this appointment and having brought his Department into contempt, it becomes a matter for the Government and not for the Minister. The Government cannot wash their hands of the blame in this matter by leaving it entirely to the Minister for Posts and Telegraphs.

Mr O'Leary: Did you not make your brother Coras Iompair Eireann manager?

Mr Lemass: No.

Minister for Posts and Telegraphs (Mr Everett): The difficulties which have arisen in filling the sub-post-mastership of Baltinglass arise from a decision of mine in 1948. Some time after I became Minister for Posts and Telegraphs, I instructed my Department that, in future, sub-offices should not be transferred to relatives except when the applicant was the husband, wife, son, daughter, brother, sister, widower or widow of the outgoing sub-post-master. Before that, sub-offices could be transferred at the option of the retiring sub-postmaster to a wider range of relatives. I saw, and see, no reason whatsoever why sub-postmasterships, unlike all other public appointments in the State, should be handed on by inheritance. I did not, however, make a complete break with the previous practice, as I felt it might be unfair to serving postmasters and, accordingly, I permitted transfer to immediate relatives. That decision was given by me in December, 1948, and I informed the sub-postmasters' union of it at an interview with them shortly afterwards.

Yesterday, I stated specifically at Question Time that it was I who had made this decision. My predecessor in office should be well aware, from this experience as Minister, that the application of the old regulation gave rise to grave difficulties.

Mr Little: I am not aware of it.

Mr Everett: The Deputy knew there was bargaining and that money passed between people.

Mr Little: I knew nothing of the sort.

Mr Everett: It must have come to the Deputy's knowledge.

Mr Little: There are difficulties, no matter what regulation one makes.

111

Mr Everett: A person could not transfer the postmastership unless someone was getting money from it and we were not in a position to say whether this was happening or not.

Mr Little: You were not forced to do it.

Mr Everett: The sub-postmistress of Baltinglass tendered her resignation on 14 April last and accordingly the post was advertised. I should like to stress that this was done as a routine matter by my Department without any previous consultation with me. There were two candidates. One was Miss H.H. Cooke, the niece of the retiring sub-postmistress. She had been working in the office as assistant since 1936. The other candidate was Mr M.T. Farrell.

Both were good candidates. Miss Cooke has a satisfactory record as assistant and I do not wish to say anything which would appear to cast a reflection on her. The fact that she was an assistant confers no entitlement on her to appointment as sub-postmistress. Practically every day, and long before my time, assistants have been passed over in favour of other candidates. The strongest point, however, in Miss Cooke's favour, so far as I can judge from the arguments put forward, was that members of her family had held the office over a long period of years. It seems to be argued that she should, therefore, have been automatically appointed. My inclination, frankly, was in the opposite direction. This family has held the sub-office over a long period of years. Miss Cooke is not an immediate relative of the outgoing sub-postmistress and it did not seem unreasonable that the benefits of the employment should now go elsewhere in the event of another candidate, at least as good as Miss Cooke, offering. I consider Mr Farrell to be a better candidate.

Mr T. Brennan: The people of Baltinglass do not think so.

Mr Everett: On all the usual grounds of character, financial stability, etc., he is a good candidate. He is at least 30 years younger than the other candidate, he has had a college education and has given much voluntary service to his country. He became a lieutenant in the LDF and Deputy Brennan was his district leader.

Mr T. Brennan: I am giving him all credit for being a member of the LDF. There were several others as well as he *[sic]*.

Mr Everett: In the LDF days Deputy Brennan was supporting a recruiting drive and promising that preference would be given to members of the Defence Forces seeking Government employment. This young man is still a member of the FCA and was highly recommended for the position of sub-postmaster by his commanding officer. I might mention that Mr Farrell was also recommended to the Department by at least four Fianna Fáil T.D.s and Senators.

Mr Lemass: That was the deciding factor?

Mr Everett: You cannot have it both ways. He was recommended by four prominent members of the Fianna Fáil Party.

Mr Lemass: Name them.

Mr Everett: The Fianna Fáil Party is right, no matter which candidate is successful. They back both horses. I, however, had to take a decision as between these people and, on mature reflection, I regarded it as my duty to give the position to a person about whose qualifications I had no doubt whatsoever and who had served in his country's forces during the emergency. This step, I feel, will encourage other men in similar positions, and will let them see that the promises given to them on recruitment are not being broken.

I make no apology for giving preference to a young man like Mr Farrell, anxious to secure employment in this country, in preference to another person who, while in no way personally objectionable would, in the natural course of things, probably be retiring from office in another ten years or so.

With the development, during this Government's term of office of the various Post Office services, particularly the telephone service, greatly increased demands are being made on postmasters' efficiency, and, bearing this in mind, I am anxious that appointments to that class should be given to active young people wherever it is reasonably practicable to do so. Another motive which I have in doing this is to give young men and women an opportunity of making a home and a livelihood for themselves in their own country. I do not agree that because a grandmother had held a semi-

113

Government job only her relations in this generation have the right to the job, notwithstanding that other citizens may have better qualifications. I was never in favour of the closed trade policy which debars a man from a living simply because his father had not a similar one.

Reference has been made to the expenditure involved in changing the office from the present building to the new one. Such expenditure is normal in practically every sub-office appointment and while it could have been avoided had I selected Miss Cooke, I would not be prepared to let that consideration influence me in turning down the better candidate. As Mr Farrell may be expected to hold the office for a long period, the amount involved is a very small capital charge. As regards representations made by the local people, I have considered those. I am not sure that they are altogether disinterested and I feel quite confident that, if the people in the Baltinglass area as a whole had an opportunity to make their wishes known in the matter, Mr Farrell would be supported by at least as strong a body of opinion as that which supports the other candidate.

According to the Official Debates, Vol. 123, No. 9, column 1384, for last Wednesday, Deputy Cogan put the following questions: – 'Is the Minister aware that the business has been transferred now to a public house, which has been the headquarters of the Minister's Party in West Wicklow and that the position has been given to the son of a county councillor, a member of the Minister's Party?'

I wish to take this opportunity of making it clear to the House that the allegations in that question are incorrect. Mr Farrell's premises where the Post Office business will be transacted is a draper's shop and not a public house. Mr Farrell's premises was not my Party's headquarters. All our meetings were held in the local cinema. Anyone who knows me knows also from my record that I am a bad supporter of the publicans. Again, it is not true to say that the position has been given to the son of a county councillor, a member of my Party. Mr Farrell, Senior, is not a member of the county council. At least, Deputy Cogan owes it to the House, if not to me, to give the facts of the case.

Mr Lemass: He was a councillor until the last election.

Mr Everett: I have no apology to offer for making the decision. I am taking full responsibility for it. The person was qualified and if Deputies require the names of the four Fianna Fáil representatives who supported him, they are Deputies Davern and Bob Ryan; Senators Andy Fogarty and S. Hayes.

Mr Lemass: On a point of privilege, is the Minister attempting to suggest that, in making appointments of this kind, he is influenced by recommendations from members of the Dáil or Seanad?

An Ceann Comhairle: That is not a point of privilege.

Mr Lemass: It does not make it any the less a dirty job.

An Ceann Comhairle: It is not a point of privilege, on which the Deputy ostensibly arose.

Mr Cogan rose.

An Ceann Comhairle: I will not hear any more about the question.

ON THE SAME day, The O'Mahoney wrote to the Taoiseach, and threatened to resign his chairmanship of Fine Gael. From his sick bed too, the parish priest of Baltinglass, Fr Doyle, dictated a letter to James Everett. It carried his conviction that a grave injustice had been done in appointing Michael Farrell and asked the Minister to bring the matter to a hasty conclusion. A new protester reported for protest duty, Mrs Daphne Lawlor. Delighted newsmen discovered that this lady was a cousin of the wife of the reigning King of England, George VI.

Helen Cooke's supporters had become pleased with the support they were receiving from those they would have called 'the gentry'. This latest support brought more valuable attention from the press. It also dealt Michael Farrell's supporters a valuable card and they played it immediately. Anti-British feeling and resentment towards large landowners were still rife in the rural Ireland of the late 1940s, early 1950s. There was a considerable amount of bad feeling towards the British royal family and its trappings. A powerfully emotive distaste towards any connection with British imperialism existed. On the very evening of Mrs Lawlor's arrival on the picket-line, Farrell's supporters marched by torchlight to the Town Hall. 'Baltinglass wanting no truck with the Queen of England' was the theme of their placards and their speeches.

There were twelve Independents in the first Inter-Party government (1948-1951). To survive Dáil votes, the government needed the support of at least two. An Taoiseach, John A. Costello received a letter from Paddy Cogan withdrawing his support because of the Baltinglass affair. He read other condemnatory correspondence too, including that from the Church of Ireland rector in Kiltegan, Co. Wicklow. The Baltinglass Protest Committee issued a press release calling for integrity and clean administration in government. They improved their emergency call-up system, adding a watchman who sat by a telephone. The national press was making the 'Battle of Baltinglass' front page news.

On 10 December, Michael Farrell's supporters placed a picket on the school where Ben Hooper taught. Their placards demanded his removal and called on parents to take away their children. The same night, Miss Cooke's supporters received word from their intelligence sources that the disconnection of Cooke's exchange would take place early next morning and that the linesmen would be escorted by members of the Garda Síochána. Using every line in the same exchange, the committee contacted as many as possible. Throughout the night, they drove around the local area alerting others. They set off the siren at 7.15 and rang a hand bell. The crowd gathered. General Dennis appealed for a non-violent protest. Then the Gardaí came and were surprised that the Baltinglass protesters knew of their secretly planned operation. Neither side seemed too sure what to do. Another Baltinglass priest, Fr Mahoney, asked the Garda Superintendent to hold everything until he found out if his sick parish priest had heard from the Taoiseach. He went to Fr Doyle's house and the letter had just arrived. The Taoiseach supported his Minister's decision. The morning dragged on, a miserable morning of sleet and spitting snow. General Dennis and others went to Farrell's and asked Mrs Farrell to request her son to withdraw. She refused. They asked Farrell himself and he too refused. Ben Farrell, Michael's father, was also resolute.

Neither the Gardaí nor the protesters wanted trouble. The former placed a cordon across the street, the latter sounded their siren again. Reinforcements arrived and got through the cordon by saying they were on their way to work. Their work was strengthening the picket line. Some of them wanted action, however, and their leaders feared an outbreak of violence, especially when the police drove a truck along the path and forced them off the celebrated slab! The Gardaí forcibly removed others who were not in the truck's way.

If Miss Cooke's defending troops were momentarily dispersed, she herself locked the Post Office door. The only one she admitted was an English reporter whose paper called him at the office at the same time every day. Outside, the linesmen prepared to raise the slab and disconnect her, in spite of jeers from the crowd. Deputy Cogan then arrived.

He gave a spirited speech. Others did too. Women arrived bearing black flags while others drew blinds in windows, pronouncing mourning for the cause everyone thought was lost.

> Now all the countryside joined in, the lowly and the great;
> There were elephant-guns from Poona, and pikes from '98.
> But the Coosacks came from Dublin, and the Irish Navy too,
> And poor Cooke, she burnt her fingers on this wretched Irish stew.

Michael Farrell's men then marched up the street, carrying a national flag. Linesmen completed the disconnection of Miss Cooke's exchange. Later, the next day's mail was delivered to Farrell's. The 'Battle of Baltinglass' seemed to be over. Miss Cooke thought so and decided to emigrate to England. General Dennis persuaded her to remain a while. Over the following days picketing continued outside the school where Ben Hooper taught. This drew some attention

117

from the newspapers, but reporters were beginning to leave Baltinglass. They had not reckoned with the military man in charge of the protest committee.

Against the wishes of the committee, maverick protesters chopped down telegraph poles outside Baltinglass, in Ballinure, near Grangecon. With its approval, others bought rubber stamps bearing the legend: Baltinglass Demands Clean Administration. They franked mail with them in a make-shift Post Office at O'Neill's, a shop licensed to sell stamps.

They boycotted the new Post Office at Farrell's. Incoming mail, however, arrived at Farrell's. Postmen delivered a large volume of it to Miss Helen Cooke, because letters of sympathy and support were coming from all over Ireland and from abroad. Some protesters wanted to apply to have their telephones disconnected. Others urged using them more and more to cause confusion at Farrell's. The takings at the new office were discussed in the Dáil. Paddy Cogan used the opportunity to elicit information on the TDs and Senators who had recommended Farrell's appointment. They were Jack McQuillan, E. Rooney, J. Davern, R. Ryan, Oliver Flanagan, Senators A. Fogarty and S. Hayes. Note: Mr Davern later said, on 14 December:

> My recommendation was made in response to a request by an FCA officer who asked me for it on the grounds that another FCA officer was an applicant ... I do not know Mr Farrell ... I had no idea that this appointment would be the cause of depriving a lady who had 14 years' faithful service behind her of her position ... in any case I find it hard to believe that a recommendation from one or other members of the Fianna Fáil Party was the determining consideration with the Minister responsible for the making of this recommendation.

Cogan also asked the Minister if he was aware that Oliver Flanagan was claiming that he had got Farrell the appointment by threatening to reveal two scandals involving the Labour Party. There was further argument and more commotion in the House. Next day, Cogan brought up the matter of the vocational school picket and the Cheann

Comhairle threatened to name him before he withdrew, shouting further accusations.

In Baltinglass, General Dennis still hankered about the idea of the aeroplane dropping leaflets. This could be useful if the protest moved onto a national platform. Dennis made a deal with a former Royal Air Force pilot, Norman Ashe. Dennis had discovered that it was illegal to drop leaflets, but the pilot fixed a public address system to his plane, fitted a silencer and took off. His voice could not be heard in O'Connell Street where the picket below waved to him. But flying low over the Dublin suburbs, and Bray and Wicklow, people heard his demand for clean administration and his urgent pleas to support Miss Helen Cooke. His catch-call was, of course, 'Baltinglass Calling'. In the city centre, Dublin citizens warmly received the Baltinglass picket outside the General Post Office, a building associated with another minority fight against the establishment. Placards displayed carried slogans like 'You may be thrown out of your job next' or 'Our Fight is your Fight – we ask your support'. In his Dáil office, the secretary of another government party, Clann na Poblachta, read a letter from Patrick O'Grady of the party's Baltinglass branch. It outlined the case for Miss Cooke, deplored the government stand and stated that his branch of the party was dissolved. O'Grady's letter ended with the sentence, 'The days of the Land League are back'.

In the Dáil, the controversy still continued, with the Deputies who had recommended Farrell defending their action amid heckling and hurled abuses. The cutting of telegraph poles spread, and on at least one occasion, the unknown hewers of wood isolated Baltinglass completely. People all over the country were debating the issue in bars, on the streets and in the letters columns of the newspapers. Some of these touched on sensitive nerves. At an Athlone Urban District Council meeting, F.J. Waters, County Councillor, and A. Faulkner congratulated the people of Baltinglass on their 'democratic stand against bureaucracy'.

Eventually, Helen Cooke gave her own viewpoint. She wrote to the papers saying that her character had been

119

taken. The interest being taken in the case was apparent when front pages commented on the letter being carried inside. Miss Cooke added a type of preface: 'I have waited some considerable time hoping there might be found one man in the camp that was willing to forego place and pension in order that he might defend justice. My character has been taken away where I was unable to defend it'. She never thought, she said, 'that Holy Ireland would fall so low'. She censured the government and made a startling claim. The parish priest, one curate, bank managers, solicitors and other prominent people, as well as 90% of the shopkeepers in Baltinglass had signed her application form, but when some of the committee had inspected it recently, only one recommendation was attached. Mr Farrell's backers, on the other hand, 'were increased to numerous ones, including two T.Ds.' (There has been no explanation as to how Miss Cooke knew that Farrell's application had had only two recommendations origi- nally.) The committee of townspeople were also informed, Miss Cooke complained, that Farrell's appointment was made three weeks previously. 'Head office was informed the day before I was, namely 23 November 1950. Why did it take three weeks for my letter to go to Naas?'

Miss Cooke quoted Department regulations against using licensed premises. She outlined her considerable education and involvement with the Republican Press Office during the War of Independence. The healthy turnover at her Post Office merited mention before she dropped a clever piece of information. When the under- ground cable into her premises was laid, Post Office officials sought a guarantee that she would never resign, she claimed. That was because of the expense involved. Later, a letter to the press from J.P. Brennan T.D. demanded an answer from the Minister to Helen Cooke's letter.

The Defence Committee organised a single-day tele- phone boycott, during which people travelled to other Post Office areas to make phone calls. Their leader was not making calls that day. Instead, Major General Dennis was working on his secret weapon. It needed only pen and ink and a disputed postal service, but was to be the most powerful of all munitions marshalled for the 'Battle of Baltinglass'.

Dennis was landlord of both Farrell's and Cooke's. He wrote as follows to the Taoiseach and sent copies to the newspapers:

As you have consistently refused to see me or to receive a deputation from Baltinglass on the question of the appointment by your Minister for Posts and Telegraphs of Mr Michael Farrell to the position of Sub-Postmaster, I feel it my duty to write to you.

The merits of Miss Cooke's qualifications must by now be well known to you, as well as the strength of feeling in the country on the question, and I do not intend to go into them in this letter. But you may have formed the impression that I have some personal antagonism to Mr Farrell and his family. This is far from being the case. Mr Everett, being a close personal friend of the family, must be well aware that not long ago, I, as Mrs Farrell's landlord, was in a position to give her considerable help in the matter of her lease, and that I willingly gave that help to a family whom I have known since childhood, and with whom neither my father nor I have ever been on other than friendly terms. My personal feelings have only been aroused by the grave wrong that I see being done to Miss Katie Cooke in her old age, and to her niece who has served the State honourably and without fault for many years. From your only public statement, it would appear that you have set your face against any form of public inquiry, and have accepted the statements of the Minister for Posts and Telegraphs, some of which do, in fact, require corroboration.

Mr Everett has stated in the Dáil, in answer to a question, that 'not the majority' of the people of Baltinglass are fighting for the rights of Miss Cooke. If he is sincere in this belief, he has been badly misinformed, and I suggest that he should take a referendum of the postal area served by the Baltinglass Post Office. Mention has been made on his behalf, if not by him, of suitability of premises. The old Post Office has been most suitable for over 70 years. The new one is installed in a licensed premises. The whole of this premises is covered by the licence, and, as landlord, I believe I am entitled to object to any restriction of the licence which must, of necessity, reduce the value of my property.

He has also stated that the appointment was made on grounds of character and financial stability. Comparisons of this nature are objectionable, and it would be neither right nor proper for me to discuss them.

You may feel that to have given way to the protest made in Baltinglass would have been a submission to mob law, and would have created an unfortunate precedent. We are only too well aware from the history of this country that mob law results inevitably from misrule. Our democratic machinery gives us the right to elect our own government to rule over our affairs; if it fails in that task, or if misrule creeps in, the people must speak out.

The question of the appointment of the sub-postmaster in a small village would be a matter of little consequence in these tremendous days in which we live, were it not that it has brought up the whole principle of clean administration, and hits right at the roots of democratic government.

While the letter was on its way to the Taoiseach and to national newspapers, its author called to Farrell's, accompanied by his solicitor. The solicitor told Mrs Farrell that she had broken her lease by carrying out structural alterations. While assuring her that he had no intention of concluding their agreement, Dennis pointed out that she was devaluing the property by excluding a portion of it from its licence.

More poles were cut down. On 16 December the main cable to the town was severed halfway between Cooke's and Farrell's. A written plea to his parishioner from Fr Doyle ended the practice. Farrell supporters still marched and delivered reasoned speeches. Letters continued to arrive on editors' desks.

A DUBLIN LADY started a branch of the Cooke protest committee. In no time, Treasa McGeehan was swamped with letters and visits from people vowing support. On 18 December, the Women Writers Club of Ireland, at its annual dinner in the Hibernian Hotel, Dublin, signed a protest. Kate O'Brien, chairman, urged all members to speak out against 'jobbery and corruption evident in Irish legislation today'. Kathleen Lynn Doyle, Dr Lorna Reynolds and Dr Mary Macken also spoke. A celebrity of the period, Eoin 'The Pope' O'Mahony arrived on the scene. This eccentric genealogist, lecturer and barrister was more widely known as a raconteur. (The learned, Cork-born Knight of Malta and Georgian Society member was wont to arrive unannounced into interesting gatherings, and stay as long as he wished. The nearest guess to the origin of his nickname suggested that, when a schoolboy in Clongowes Wood

College, he made a statement that his friends, mistakenly, took to be an expressed ambition to be Pope.) O'Mahoney met and talked but the pontifical input to the 'Battle of Baltinglass' amounted only to a few newspaper reports and an offer to Helen Cooke to give up and run for the Dáil in a Cork constituency, with The Pope as her election agent. How could she lose?

Felix O'Neill, chairman of West Wicklow Fine Gael, resigned from that office. The O'Mahoney resigned from the party too. In a letter to General Richard Mulcahy, Fine Gael leader, he said, 'I tried very hard to make justice victorious, but justice has been completely ignored. You personally should know that I could never stand for anything of this kind, and I am more than amazed that full support has not been given by Fine Gael to Miss Cooke.'

There were reports that up to six government-supporting deputies were contemplating resignation. A Clann na Poblachta County Convention in Westmeath called for Mr Everett's resignation. Two of Miss Cooke's Post Office assistants took up other employment. Michael Farrell spoke more frequently; in the main, he claimed having more support in the area than Helen Cooke. So the protest committee sought signatures and claimed an 87% majority. On the night of 21 December, despite the busy Christmas period, they met in Felix O'Neill's to double-check the signatures. There was quietness as they carefully perused each vote. Mr O'Neill left the room, came back in a short while and stood looking at the others. Two of them began arguing about an incorrect tally and almost missed Felix O'Neill's unemotional statement.

'Farrell resigned.'

Felix had heard on the radio what Miss Cooke's supporters had been unaware of. The nation knew it before most of the people of Baltinglass. The news did not make the next morning's editions, but Michael Farrell's dignified letter of resignation and the Minister's reply appeared on 23 December. The front page of the *Irish Press* carried them:

Baltinglass, Co. Wicklow
20th Dec., 1950

Dear Mr Everett,

I am exceedingly sorry that my appointment as Sub-postmaster of Baltinglass has caused so much controversy and that it has been utilised by your political opponents and certain misguided people to launch an unwarranted attack on you, personally and politically.

My family and I appreciate so much the sterling services which, as a public representative, you have rendered to the nation in general, and to the County Wicklow in particular, that these attacks upon you have caused us much pain and anxiety. I desire to assure you that I would not consciously be the cause of unleashing against you the bitterness and vituperation that has been deliberately directed against you in such unmeasured terms during the past few weeks.

As you know, I was an officer in the LDF during the Emergency and am at present an officer of the FCA. I hold testimonials from my superior officers (who, incidentally, recommended me for the Baltinglass post) which express in high terms their regard for my service and efficiency. It is an honour to me to wear an Irish officer's uniform and to be privileged to serve my country in any danger that may arise. Holding these views, therefore, I am particularly anxious that the uniform which I proudly wear should not become associated with, or be in any way besmirched by, the violent abuse and illegal acts for which your political opponents have been responsible following my appointment.

Having reviewed the whole position I have now come to the conclusion that I should resign my position as Sub-Postmaster of Baltinglass in order that my name and my family's will not be further used as a cover from which to launch base and undeserved attacks upon you and so that, as an officer in the nation's Defence Forces, I may not even remotely appear to associate my status with the brawling atmosphere in which certain persons delight.

I hope you will forgive me for taking this decision, but, believe me, I have been actuated solely by my high regard for you, my appreciation for your unstinted service to the people of the County Wicklow and for the honour of my uniform. I know it looks odd that I am eligible to wear the uniform of the Defence Forces of my own country, and am free to die in its service, but am denied an appointment to a small position in a country sub-Post Office. However, one must not expect logic when abuse and vilification have taken control of the situation. I thank you for your confidence in me and I close by again tendering my deep regret that you should be occasioned such worry and annoyance.

Yours sincerely,
Michael Farrell

Dublin,
21st December, 1950

Dear Mr Farrell,

I have received your letter of the 20th instant tendering your resignation from the position of sub-Postmaster of Baltinglass. I regret that you have taken this decision, but I appreciate your sentiments and the manly spirit which actuated you. I should like you to understand clearly that from the standpoint of qualifications, you were eminently fitted for the post, and that your decision to resign is in no way related to your ability and general suitability for the position. As your decision is your own free choice, I must accept it as such.

I should perhaps add that your appointment has thrown into bold relief the long-established practice of making appointments to these posts. For some time past I have been considering, with my Department, the adoption of a new method of selecting candidates for such appointments. The present method, which we inherited from our predecessors, is open to many objections, inasmuch as it provides opportunities for candidates to seek political influence in respect of such appointments, as is evidenced by the fact that even in your own case members of parties supporting the government, and four members of the Fianna Fáil Party, felt impelled to make representations to me on your behalf. Ironically enough the Deputies of the Fianna Fáil Party complained when the candidate whom they recommended was appointed.

I dislike intensely a system of appointment where political influence can be used in the filling of such positions and I intend at the earliest opportunity to introduce arrangements whereby appointments to sub-Post Offices will be made be an official interview board which will be instructed to disqualify at once any candidate who attempts to use political influence in the furtherance of his or her candidature.

Yours sincerely,
James Everett

There was no triumphalism. Some drinks, of course, but no public show of celebration. Indeed, if the truth were known, more than a few may have felt sorry for Michael Farrell. There was considerable disapproval of using 'the gentry' to arbitrate in a dispute between ordinary folk. More, the community had split and it would take a long time for this severe wound to heal, if it should ever heal. Michael

Farrell claimed that his supporters were against his decision to resign. He refused to consider any alternative position, if such was offered. Business in his Post Office improved as consultation took place about a government regulation stipulating three months' notice of resignation. On Saturday, 23 December 1950, the *Irish Press* also reported:

BALTINGLASS AWAITS THE NEXT MOVE

Staffed by GPO trained personnel, Baltinglass Post Office transacted business yesterday when Mr Michael Farrell, who has resigned as Postmaster, was in charge. Post Office regulations provide that a sub-postmaster must give three months notice of his intention to resign. It was stated authoritatively yesterday that the vacancy would be advertised and the appointment made by an official interview board, 'Which will be instructed to disqualify at once any candidate who attempts to use political influence in the furtherance of his or her candidature'.

The townspeople of Baltinglass spent a quiet day yesterday recovering from the major surprise created by the sudden resignation of Mr Farrell who, for eleven days, had held the position. This was the main topic of conversation in the town which was more than usually thronged for a fair day, as well as for Christmas shopping. Newspapers were eagerly sought by inhabitants as soon as the morning bus brought them in.

Meanwhile, Miss Cooke still needed her protest committee. After all, she still had not got her job back. There was a flurry of correspondence to the newspapers. Most of the names in the controversy to date re-appeared. On Saturday 30 December under a headline 'Baltinglass Reaches Out to Provinces', the *Irish Press* said:

Baltinglass Protest Committee, fighting the claim of Miss Helen Cooke to be Postmistress, began their campaign yesterday morning when two car-loads of

126

speakers set out on a four-day tour. The destinations of the cars, which left yesterday morning were Cork and Galway, but meetings will be held at most of the principal towns en route, and house to house canvasser signatures will be made in some of them. Leaders of the groups which left yesterday were Messrs P. Sheridan, F. Doyle and F. O'Neill.

Four additional cars are due to leave Baltinglass tomorrow on a tour of centres within a 30 to 40 mile radius, and a number of other cars will leave on Monday. All cars are equipped with a public address system

Miss Cooke will be again an applicant for the position of Postmistress and has written for an application form.

The Dublin branch of the protest committee have now received 7,000 signatures for their memorial on behalf of Miss Cooke. Yesterday's mail was the heaviest yet received.

The public protest meeting which was to have been held in the Mansion House, Dublin on January 5th, has been postponed to a date to be announced later. A sub-committee of the Baltinglass Protest Committee was formed in Collinstown, Co. Westmeath last night, and Mr B. O'Donnell was appointed Honorary Secretary. Sub-committees were also formed in Kilkenny and Waterford.

Throughout the country, because the affair had taken a firm hold of the nation, the call-sign 'Baltinglass Calling' rang out in towns and cities. The government was under fire from Old IRA, leading articles and leading dignitaries. Advertisements appeared in the newspapers seeking applicants for the Baltinglass Post Office position. Miss Cooke applied, though not through the local Post Office at Farrell's, where notice of the vacancy appeared.

On 26 January 1951 the Naas postmaster called to Miss Cooke and informed her that her application for sub-postmistress in Baltinglass had been successful. He called on Michael Farrell too and told him the news. In spite of a reference to procedures in Mr Everett's letter accepting Michael Farrell's signature earlier, there had been no interview.

IN EVERY BAR over every drink people teased out the pros and cons of the affair that provided a topic of conversation and argument right into the spring and after.

On 22 February 1951, Cogan asked the Minister for Justice, Seán MacEoin about the number of gardaí involved in Baltinglass during the line-laying work and the cost of sending them there. MacEoin would not give the figures, but he outlined the cost at £19.9.7 for Transport and £20.10.6 for subsistence. Moreover, from 12-16 February, extra Gardaí in the area had cost £35.17.9 for transport and £87.12.0 for subsistence.

By then, the government was involved in another controversy when the Minister for Health Dr Noel Browne (Clann na Poblachta), resigned. He had published his 'Mother and Child Scheme', irrespective of colleagues' calls for including a means test. An April meeting of bishops rejected the scheme and the government succumbed to their wishes. Between Baltinglass and Maynooth, the Taoiseach, John A. Costello had had enough. He dissolved the Dáil and Fianna Fáil won the subsequent election. Gaffney, the balladeer had been ignored, perhaps foolishly:

> The case has gone to U.N.O. and we're waiting for the day
> When Truman, Attlee and MacBride will come along and say:
> 'Get back behind your parallel, drop atom bombs and gas
> And respect the boundaries and the laws of Sovereign Baltinglass.'

POSTSCRIPT

Over a year later, on 21 February 1952, Deputy Cogan asked a Dáil question about the state of the Garda barracks in Baltinglass. He made the remark that the force 'now resides in a historic ruin'. Quick as a flash, Oliver Flanagan quipped, 'Is the Post Office a historic ruin?' but Cogan had the last word: 'There is another ruin there. Your name is on that.'

Baltinglass Post Office passed on to Felix O'Neill in the early 1960s. Peter Murphy took over in 1966 and Simon Murphy in 1986.

THE SINGER, NOT THE STAMPS

Bratislavian Paul Singer was born into a Jewish family on 31 July 1911, five months after 750,000 people attended the funeral of his namesake, the German socialist leader. In 1936 the family moved to Austria. Paul was educated in Vienna and later in London, Paris and Switzerland. At Lausanne, he won a doctorate in social and political science. Probably in anticipation of events to come in Germany and Austria, the Singers moved again in 1930, this time to London. Paul studied economics and international law there for a while before joining his father's (Auriel) finance company. In 1940, Paul met Irma Wolf, daughter of a London businessman. The couple married in February 1946. He became a British citizen and conducted a trading business that failed. In 1953, his father's business, with Paul now a director, collapsed. Its liabilities reached £45,000. Early in 1954, Singer moved his family to Dublin. He met up with a respectable Dun Laoghaire auctioneering firm run by the Shanahan family. Jerome Shanahan was 56 years of age; his son, Arthur Desmond, was 29. They dealt mainly in antiques at their auction-rooms where weekly sales took place. Singer discussed a new idea with the Shanahans and on 12 October of that year, a company was incorporated under the name Shanahan's Stamp Auctions Ltd. Its original shareholders and directors were Paul Singer, his wife, 31 year-old Irma, Jerome Shanahan and Arthur Desmond Shanahan. The enterprise started from an investment of £100 each from Singer and Jerome Shanahan.

Imposing, well-dressed, dark-haired, bearded and nearly 20 stone, Singer impressed. A nervous tic might have conveyed a somewhat sinister impression were it not for his confident air and apparent knowledge of philately. As soon as he made the deal with the Shanahans, he took off to London and bought one minor collection of stamps. Auctioned the following week in Corrig Avenue, Dun Laoghaire, it returned a modest profit.

The company continued to grow. Quite simply, it bought stamps and sold them by auction. Purchasing funds came from the public. Promotional literature and advertisements expressed entitlement to a return of monies contributed and, under certain conditions, profits. The deal seemed to be watertight. It amazed the public and 30,000 people, mostly from Dublin, got involved. Investment in philately was a novelty in Ireland but, being a nation of gamblers, many small investors responded to attractive offers that the company made in newspaper advertisements.

There was also *Green I.S.L.E. Philately,* a cheaply produced magazine. The initials represented 'Ireland's Stamp Lovers' Edition'. Even its paper was green. It gave Dublin and Belfast addresses and sold for one shilling. In the first issue of 22 September 1954, Paul Singer offered his editorial:

Dear Readers, here, there and everywhere,

Here is our Baby, the new magazine about which we have spoken so much. To us, the spiritual parents, it looks beautiful, but what do you think of it, stern Uncles and Aunts?

But before you pass judgement, let us tell you what we want to make of *Green I.S.L.E. Philately.* We want it to be not only instructive but enjoyable also. We want it to be pleasant not only to the specialist, but also to the layman who has a vague interest in philately. We chose articles not only for their philatelic but also for their entertainment value.

Have we succeeded? Probably not. Because – and now we must let you into our dark secret – we have no journalistic experience whatsoever. We are learning as we go. And we are relying on your advice. Tell us what you like, what you don't like, what you want added, what you want omitted. Be outspoken, be rude, but tell us what you really think of *Green I.S. L. E. Philately.*

We shall take every advice into consideration and we promise you one thing – issue Number 2 will be better than issue No. 1, and issue No. 3 will be better than issue No. 2, and so on. (No wisecracks, please, about skipping the next 23 issues and continuing with issue No. 25.)

Anyhow, dear friends, philatelic and otherwise, we have met with so much encouragement, consideration and help from you all in the past that we face our journalistic future not only

131

with trepidation but also with great hope, because we know that a friendly readership is half the battle.

Now friends, take a comfortable chair, put your slippers on, take a glass of milk (or whatever else you take as a nightcap) and begin to read. We shall anxiously watch out for a happy smile on your face.

There was a feature called 'Philatelic Horrors' and one on 'A Woman in Stamp Land'. Singer showed that he was establishing important contacts, like the highly popular and charitable Lord Mayor of Dublin, Alfie Byrne, who wrote in that first issue of *Green I.S.L.E. Philately*:

I would like to be amongst the many who will wish to congratulate you.

The reason why I rejoice particularly in your efforts is that here again is a field where Ireland should and now certainly will show its independence from the outside world.

Let your magazine show the world the Irish spirit in philately. Let the world know that we, too, have great specialists and that we can make our contribution to this hobby of hobbies, to this Golden Chain of International Peace and Friendship.

Please send me your magazine regularly as I am anxious to follow your progress.

Alfie Byrne was one of many prominent personalities who fell for Singer's charm. While the ebullient doctor cultivated and cajoled the wealthy and the intellectual, however, his main target was the modest investor. He satisfied his own ego by his upper-class acquaintances, but he realised that his bread and butter would come from the man and woman in the street. In a way, it motivated people in the same way as pools or giant draws. The possibility of a coup for a relatively small outlay always attracts.

Singer's magazine offered advice to stamp buyers. Issue No. 2 carried the editorial headline, 'You Have Smiled!!' Smiles certainly appeared on one face – Singer's! He continued hob-nobbing with Dublin's social set, but he had his finger firmly on the pulse of popular opinion.

Advertising in the magazine included Shanahan's normal auction business and other stamp-dealing businesses in Ireland and England. It invited suggestions and criticism and even hinted at publishing a book of these, with profit-sharing among the writers. The editorial's thrust was towards friendly co-operation and showing the way to amateur philatelists and small investors. For example, its chatty content announced the wedding of 'our popular auctioneer, Mr Desmond Shanahan' to Diana, daughter of E.T. O'Sullivan, which would take place on 22 September 1954. A later edition reported on the reception at Kilcroney Hotel, Bray, Co. Wicklow, and honeymoon in Paris. It said, 'We feel sure that you all will want to join us in wishing the happy couple the best of luck for their joint future and may they provide Ireland with many little stamp collectors'.

The magazine included a catalogue and a postal bid-ding form. The former explained what was on offer and estimated the price each lot might reach in the next auction. On the latter, customers stated the amount they wished to spend and if they were agreeable to transfer amounts saved on one lot towards the purchase of another that exceeded the agreed maximum.

Facilities were offered for postal viewing for customers who lived more than ten miles from Dublin. At that time, the Irish Hospitals Sweepstake was flourishing. A considerable amount of their business arrived in the post. Contemporaries of Shanahan's have stated that the stamp auction postbags were almost as full as those for the Sweepstake offices. Within a short space of time, Singer had become a name almost feared in the world of stamps. He had learned his trade quickly and his natural flair for publicity helped the progress of his business. It has to be said too that he pursued his objectives vigorously, and many customers were extremely satisfied with the returns on their investments.

The stamp auction firm drew a reasonably modest commission and everybody seemed to be happy. Soon the magazine adopted a larger format.

After one year's trading, Paul Singer was claiming that Shanahan's was the third largest philately business in Britain and Ireland. He believed at this time that he could out-deal the best in Europe. In order to profit more from this expertise, he launched a new scheme. He asked investors to subscribe £50 in Shanahan's for a minimum period of three months. That took care of the buying and Singer launched a mini-tourist drive to woo European buyers to 'this lovely land' for a profitable weekend buying his firm's stamps. So, with the bulk sums received, Singer bought keenly and sold his purchases at the Corrig Avenue auctions. Through this method he promised profit without risk, perhaps up to 200%. Whatever about 200% profit, news certainly spread about investors gaining 30 and 50 per cent.

Lights began burning late in Shanahan's as investments began piling up. Singer had appealed to the smallish investor and his success spurred him to chase a few more closet gamblers. A new scheme sought investments of just £10 for four months. This would not, however, entitle the investor to named collections. Instead, he and others would be organised into syndicates and the syndicate would own the interest in certain collections. Here is how Singer described it:

PROFIT FROM STAMPS
Without Risk
Stamps mean different things to different people.
What can they mean to you?

If your problem is a small Capital which you want to invest with absolute security, but with an unusually large return, then Stamps are the solution to your problem.

We give you the opportunity to invest small amounts from £10 upwards and participate (without overhead expenses) in the large profits attended to Stamp trading and that with our absolute guarantee for the safety of your Capital.

Your money will be outstanding for a maximum period of four months. During this period we shall buy, in your name in Britain and on the Continent, Stamps which WE KNOW will fetch higher prices in our own Auctions here. The Stamps would be invoiced to you direct and treated by us as your property.

134

These Stamps will then be entered in our next available Auction. You will be advised of your lot numbers and after the Sale we publish the results in Green I.S.L.E. Philately.

A few weeks after the Sale, but definitely not later than four months after your investment, you will recieve our cheque for your Capital and Profits.

And remember your Capital is ABSOLUTELY GUARANTEED by us and will be returned to you intact, whatever else happens.

This proposition has been tried out many times and our friends have ALWAYS made a profit. This varied between 20% and 100% of the Capital invested. The only charge to you is our Standard rate of selling commission (minimum 10%). We don't make any charge at all for buying the Stamps for you.

If you are interested, fill in the coupon below and enclose your cheque.

YOURS SINCERELY,
SHANAHAN'S STAMP AUCTIONS LTD.
38, Corrig Avenue, Dun Laogharie.
Telephone : 83654.

....

Date.....................................

To SHANAHAN'S STAMP ACUTIONS LTD
38, Corrig Avenue,
Dun Laoghaire, Dublin.

Please find enclosed herewith my cheque for .... This amount to be used to purchase Stamps in my name from British or Continental Stamp Auctioneers. These Stamps to be suitably lotted and entered into your next available Sale. The total proceeds of the Sale of these lots (less your standard commission [minimum

10%]) to be remitted to me not later than 4 months from today. But should the net proceeds be less than my investment then you will make good any shortage.
Kindly confirm acceptance by return.

Yours faithfully,

NAME (in block letters) ....

ADDRESS..

At the back of the form, Singer posed likely customer concerns and dealt with them as follows:

QUESTION: How is is possible to buy stamps in one auction and resell them in another with a large margin of profit?

ANSWER: The value of stamps is purely in the mind of the purchaser and very large variations occur between one buyer and another. We, of course, are very well placed to know which stamps will realise the best prices in our own auctions, and can, therefore, buy accordingly.

QUESTION: Do you, then, claim that you get higher prices, than, say, London auctioneers?

ANSWER: Not necessarily. But every auctioneer has his own clientele and knows what they want. It would be quite possible and profitable, with certain stamps, to do the same operation in reverse – buy from us and sell in British and Continental auctions. The art is to know which stamps fetch higher prices here, and which fetch higher prices there. We know.

QUESTION: Why don't you do this business yourself, without offering it to outsiders?

ANSWER: We consider it unethical for an auctioneer, who should be an honest broker between buyer and seller, to offer his own ware. We also feel that his customers, both vendors and purchasers, could not have the same confidence in him if he did. We are offering this proposition to outsiders as a means of increasing our own business. We know that the more lots we offer, the more we sell to our clientele,

136

consisting of many thousands of collectors and dealers all over the world in sixty-seven countries, who have a practically unlimited purchasing power and appetite for more stamps.

Singer often bought very expensive collections, perhaps £55,000 worth. Reports of 100% profit were common. Many just broke even. Nobody lost money at this stage. There was a turnover of £1,000,000 in Shanahan's Stamp Auctions Ltd. during its early trading months. The weakness in the scheme was its very appeal. It came to the stage that, despite Singer's best efforts, there just were not enough stamps in circulation to use up the vast sums of money being offered by investors. Also, there have been suggestions that the heretofore staid world of stamp-dealing did not like Singer's flamboyant technique and cared even less for his syndicated buying and selling. If they could sell their collections elsewhere, they would not do business with him.

Under the original £50 investment scheme, the firm often bought unsold lots themselves in order to pay investors a dividend. These they would sell at a later auction. So investors seldom looked for their money back after the stipulated period. They could not do this under the syndicate scheme so, to keep customers happy, Shanahan's Stamp Auctions Ltd. allegedly began using one syndicate's money to pay another a small profit and thus win time. Despite these warning signs, the firm moved to more plush premises in George's Street, Dun Laoghaire. Although the old *Green I.S.L.E. Philately* magazine was now an expensive, glossy publication. Its green theme predominated the decor, furnishings stationery and ink in George's Street.

Singer's lifestyle improved too. In his excellent book, *Doctor of Millions* (Tralee 1965), the man whom Singer once asked to become his public relations officer, Seamus Brady, describes it:

> Singer was now living the life of an Irish lord. He had bought a magnificent mansion on a thirteen-acre estate at Foxrock, a fashionable suburb of Dublin, and christened it 'Cairn Hall'. This had formerly been the home which George Formby, the

comedian, [and ukulele player] bought as a haven of retreat for his first wife and himself on his retirement; and he had called it 'Beryldene' after his wife.

The purchase of 'Cairn Hall' was attended by the usual Singer care and caution. He did not buy the house direct. He used a company, H.B. Pipes, Ltd., in which he and his wife, Irma, held all the shares, to buy this Georgian mansion and estate on his behalf. The reason for this device has never been questioned, but it was no doubt a precaution by Singer utilising his knowledge of company law to avoid taxation.

'Cairn Hall' was breathtaking by the time Singer had furnished it to his taste. The furniture was real Chippendale antique picked up at the best auction rooms in Dublin and London. The curtains were thick velvet. There were costly paintings gracing the walls.

He had a governess for his two children. His Spanish butler, Daro, always wore a spotless white dinner jacket. A chauffeur in livery drove his big limousine. Singer, in colourful dressing gown, always breakfasted continental style on coffee and rolls in the sun patio where he could watch the artificial waterfall cascading over rocks into a pool of goldfish in his huge conservatory. But at 11 a.m. in his office he had his real breakfast: a bowl of soup, with half a dozen raw eggs. Lunch invariably was a five-course affair, the main dish being steak tartare – a pound of raw steak, minced with garlic and herbs, and bound with raw eggs. For dinner at 'Cairn Hall' caviare was always on order. And Singer drank 'black velvet', which is stout laced with champagne.

In his expensive black overcoat, steel-grey suit, but carrying a shabby brown pigskin briefcase, Singer now searched the world for stamps. He displayed a sense of humour unusual in the trade. He could be charming, testy or downright bad-tempered. On each arrival home, he stage-managed a meeting in Dublin airport. Stories spread about a group of girls from his Dun Laoghaire staff of 90 forming a welcoming party and singing *For He's a Jolly Good Fellow* when he landed. He thought this would be good for the press photographers and reporters, but they quickly tired of his antics. As he went around the world, few dealers had as much ready cash at their disposal for doing business. The auction firm lodged monies in various countries for his use. Sums included £100,000 for an American trip and £150,000 to bid for a celebrated Lombardo-Venezia collection in Milan.

The firm's annual report for 1958 was published in *The Irish Times* on 1 January 1959. It began:

SHANAHAN'S
STAMP AUCTIONS LTD.

THE CHAIRMAN REPORTS

I am very glad to be able to report to our investors about the considerable progress achieved again during the year 1958. We have now surpassed every Stamp Auctioneer in the world both as regards the value and the quality of Stamps sold during the year under review.

We held, in 1958, 23 AUCTIONS (13 in 1957) in which we sold 21,363 lots (14,977 in 1957) and our total sales realised an amount of £1,187,065 including commission (£441,559 in 1957).

During the period 1st September, 1957, to 31st August 1958, we had 9,458 'Profit from Stamps – Without Risk' Investment transactions (2,865 in 1957) which were all repaid with gains by the 31st December 1958.

The total amount invested was £846,339
(£272,002 in 1957)

The total net amount repaid was £968,775.17.7d
(£312,093 in 1957)

Giving a net Capital Gain of £122,436
(£40,091 in 1957)

This is equivalent to £14.34%
(£14.74% in 1957)

per four month period which, if left and compounded over 12 months, would give an Annual Capital Gain of approximately 50% (52% in 1957).

The report went on to say that for each four-month period, the smallest net gain was 7.5% (6% in 1957). The greatest was 31% (83% in 1957) per four month period. It listed the various plans: 'Double Barrel', 'Collection Picking' and

'Stop Loss Insurance'. These, it claimed, '(have) put us in a monopoly position, where no competitor can follow us'. Jerome Shanahan, Chairman, signed.

Paul Singer's last trip abroad to buy stamps was his most exciting. A Swiss philatelist, Maurice Burrus owned a celebrated collection valued at about £2,000,000. Singer went after it and astounded his competitors when he purchased part of the collection and obtained an option on the remainder. Reports at the time put his bid at over £300,000. The press still did not cover his flamboyant airport arrival, but they did go along to one of the biggest parties Dun Laoghaire had ever witnessed.

The Shanahan establishment in Dun Laoghaire was lavishly decorated for the event. Blown-up photographs of its directors hung on the walls of the transformed auction room in which Edmundo Ross, a popular Latin-American band from London, played for up to 600 guests. For weeks after, extravagant claims circulated. Caviare was flown in from Russia, snails and heaven knows what else from Paris. The rumours extended to private planes arriving at small airfields bearing expensive ladies of the European night!

To mark the fifth birthday of Shanahan's Stamp Auctions, there was another gigantic party. Dublin society attended, as well as Dáil deputies and the odd titled person. Reports say that Paul Singer behaved abominably, tossing around champagne bottles, pouring drinks down the fronts of ladies' dresses and being generally uncouth. Few were aware that on the same morning, 9 May 1959, his staff had discovered a robbery at George's Street, Dun Laoghaire. The Lombardo-Venezia collection had vanished. Singer told the Shanahans that the resulting publicity would make up for the loss. The scanty publicity disappointed, so Singer placed a large advertisement in the papers on 20 May:

£10,000 REWARD

After due deliberation and discussion, it has been decided that we should offer a reward of £10,000 (ten thousand) for any information leading to the discovery, in good condition of the stamps stolen during the burglary at our premises, 39 Upper Great George's St., Dun Laoghaire, Co. Dublin during the night of the 8th to 9th May.

Information leading to only partial recovery will entitle an appropriate reward. If two or more people give the same information leading to the recovery of part or whole of stamps lost, the respective reward will be shared between them.

SHANAHAN'S STAMP AUCTIONS LTD.
39, Upper Great George's Street,
Dun Laoghaire, Co. Dublin.

There was a question mark over the insurance situation. Later evidence suggests that the stamps had been insured against fire only, and not theft. Ironically, in a joke page called 'Philately Cocktail', in the most recent issue of *Green I.S.L.E. Philately*, this appeared:

> *Stamp Dealer:* Any new orders while I was out?
> *New Assistant:* Only me! Two gentlemen ordered me to put my hands up while they took away the stock.

If the keen gambling instinct of the Irish public had been instrumental in charting the success of Shanahan's Stamp Auctions Ltd., other Irish traits contributed to its downfall. A powerful cocktail of gossip, rumour and suspicion led to a gradual withdrawal of support that grew quickly to enormous proportions. Since the whole enterprise depended on using investors' money, this could have but one result. Ruin! Postbags that had contained hundreds of applications to invest now carried thousands of requests to withdraw.

Singer put the purchased English and Netherlands sections of the Burrus collection on the market. He thought this and the Reward Notice would allay investors' fears. He was wrong. The public noticed the comings and goings of policemen to the stamp auction premises and panicked all the more.

Another Irish trait, kicking a man when down, reared its ugly head. The flamboyance once admired now singled out Paul Singer for derisive comment. He had 'lost the run of himself'; He was 'having a ball on our hard earned money'. In waded the international philately circle, eager to have a go at the man who had wiped so many perforated-edged eyes. In circles where he was formerly an elitist merchant prince, Singer became a *persona non grata*.

Aspects of the stamp robbery posed questions to which the British press sought answers. Public faith in Shanahan's Stamp Auctions plummeted and on 25 May 1959 Arthur Cox and Co. solicitors announced that the directors of Shanahan's Stamp Auctions had appointed Mr Gerald W. O'Brien, a senior partner in the firm of Messrs Craig Gardner and Co., Chartered Accountants as liquidator. The liquidation was entered into on the previous 23 May. There was consternation. Estimates placed the company's assets in the region of £400,000 to £500,000. Claims from over 9,000 creditors almost reached £2,000,000, an enormous sum at the time.

The Irish Times reported:

> It is stated by the directors that the decision is not to be taken as implying insolvency. The reason this step has been taken is that, on the one hand, the company holds collections of stamps of very great value, and on the other, that large sums have been invested in the company by very numerous investors.
>
> In view of the rumours as to the solvency of the company which have been circulated, it has been considered by the directors, on legal advice, that the present step is necessary as the only way to protect and safeguard the assets of the company against precipitate demands and proceedings which would result in great injury to the investors and to her creditors as well as to the company itself. In these circumstances, it has been considered that the present step is necessary in the best interests of all concerned.
>
> The stamp auctions on May 30, June 6 and June 13 will be carried out under the supervision of the liquidator.

The newspaper added this final paragraph to the report:

Directors of the firm refused to comment yesterday. Dr Paul Singer said he could make no comment on the directors' action in going into liquidation.

THE ATTORNEY GENERAL, Andrias Ó Caoimh, however, instructed a team of detectives, led by a chief superintendent, to examine the books at Shanahan's. On 27 May, Arthur Cox and Co. announced that the firm was to petition the High Court to wind up its affairs but that this did not mean that it was bankrupt. Chief Superintendent Farrell's team were unhappy with the large amounts of money lodged abroad and with discrepancies in receipting payments from these sums for stamp collections. On 28 May, Farrell applied to Dublin District Court for four arrest warrants. These were in respect of Paul Singer, Irma Singer, Jerome Shanahan and Arthur Desmond Shanahan. Even as a stamp auction was taking place in George's Street on 29 May, Gardaí were arresting the four directors at their homes. After questioning at Dun Laoghaire Garda station, the Shanahans and Singer were driven away to a cell in the Bridewell. Word of the arrest had spread and a crowd saw them off with a verse of *For He's a Jolly Good Fellow*.

After a weekend in the Bridewell cells, the four faced District Justice Kenneth Reddin on the Monday morning. A preliminary joint charge accused them of conspiring to cheat and defraud Leo Hunt, a Sligo investor, and others. The prosecutor for the State, Walter Carroll, declared that there would be other charges, so Justice Reddin fixed bail at £100,000 for Singer, half of the sum personal, the rest independent. He also had to surrender his passport and undertake to report to the Gardaí in Dun Laoghaire every day. For Irma Singer and the two Shanahans, personal bail was fixed at £20,000 each, and the same amount in independent sureties.

Singer's solicitor, Frank Martin, applied to the High Court to seek a reduction in the bail amounts. Mr Justice Murnaghan, on 2 June, reduced Singer's personal sum to £5,000, with an independent surety of £10,000. Irma Singer's dropped to £2,000 personal, with £10,000 independent.

Jerome Shanahan's became £1,000, with an independent surety of £2,000. Arthur Desmond Shanahan's decreased bail, applied for later, was £1,000 with an independent surety of £2,000. The Shanahans easily found guarantors and Mrs Singer's father later bailed her out. During the subsequent hearing, Irma held up court proceedings for a day while she insisted on her father's bail money being invested in a National Loan at 5.25%. She got her way. Paul Singer remained in Mountjoy prison for a year and a half awaiting trial. Ulick O'Connor, who was later Arthur Desmond Shanahan's junior defence counsel, recalls that he ate 14 *fried* eggs for breakfast each morning. Mountjoy lacked the cuisine to which he was accustomed! (Other sources claimed that special food was brought in to the prison for him.)

Meanwhile Gerard O'Brien continued the liquidation process. Solicitors for investors placed claims totalling £2,000,000. They represented clients with investments from £100 to £35,000. The stamp stocks were removed to bank vaults.

OVER 300 WITNESSES gave evidence before District Justice Cathal O'Flynn during a 63-day hearing. Mr Walter Carroll prosecuted. Seán Hooper, senior counsel and Frank Martin, junior counsel, were for the Singer couple. William Fanning defended Jerome Shanahan and Ulick O'Connor appeared for his son, Arthur Desmond. The total sum of money involved in 39 charges against the accused exceeded £750,000. The charges alleged that the four accused:

> ... fraudulently intended to cheat and defraud citizens of the State by inviting them to entrust money for investment in the purchase and sale of stamps at auctions advertised in the public press, by pretending that these auctions were honestly conducted, whereas, in fact, they [the accused] knew that the moneys invested were grouped by them into syndicates, and that dividends were paid by the company on moneys invested, without reference to the prices at which stamps were sold, in that they fraudulently and deceitfully decided that dividends should be paid after auctions were held.

144

Justice O'Flynn handled the case with courtesy. Jerome Shanahan was hard of hearing and was allowed earphones connected to a microphone. Although Paul Singer might have been accused of contempt by reading a newspaper during certain early stages of the trial, the Justice allowed him join his own defence lawyers instead of issuing instructions to them from the dock. Because the Singers were Jews, he also adjourned the sitting on 15 October, the feast of Yom Kippur.

After 14 days of involved evidence regarding sales, syndicates, investments and accountancy, the State approached the second stage of its case. Here it attempted to prove that Paul Singer was over-valuing the stamps he purchased. Some of the Shanahan staff explained how Singer himself was the final arbiter on values. These men, known as 'describers' in the trade, agreed that over-valuation did take place. They also explained how unsold stamps would be reduced at every auction until, eventually, they were cleared. Two independent London assessors corroborated evidence of over-valuation and inaccurate catalogue description. One of them offered the opinion that Singer was not a philatelic expert at all.

The Shanahan staff laboriously described the method of running the business. The cashier, Hugh Finlay, attested to investments of £5,250,000 in one year when things were going well. He also alleged that well-known names in philately, as well as purely fictitious names, were used in recording fictitious sales. Of the latter, a Mr Zombie, the books showed, owed Shanahan's Stamp Auctions Ltd. over £250,000. The books also showed that the firm charged commission on invented transactions. There seemed to be a situation where Singer more or less decided the amount of profit that ought to be paid to each investor, irrespective of the trading position. The elaborate system used is described in detail in Seamus Brady's *Doctor of Millions*. Customers too testified to forged invoices and incorrect ledger entries. Then the State targeted the monies lodged abroad in Singer's name. The list was as staggering as Singer's travel itinerary.

Next for questioning was Irma Singer. She claimed that she knew nothing about stamps and was on a wage of £13 a week.

Enter the accountants, whose testimony of auction procedures was involved but edifying. The penultimate witness, an insurance broker, told how he had negotiated cover against fire in respect of the stamps. He mentioned cover against theft, but Singer and Arthur Desmond Shanahan, he said, opted to accept burglary risk themselves.

At this stage, observers felt the State had made a strong case. They met its decision to call Mrs Diana Shanahan as a final witness with disbelief. She could not testify against her husband, Arthur Desmond, so Prosecution asked the District Justice to send him for trial alone and adjourn the hearing against the other three for a fortnight. Ulick O'Connor, for Arthur Desmond, protested and sensibly pointed out the possibility of the Singers and Shanahan senior being acquitted and his client going for trial alone – despite the fact that all four were charged. The District Justice gave due consideration and refused both the adjournment and a separate trial for Shanahan junior. The prosecution then amended the charges against the four. They now read:

That between January 1, 1955, and May 23, 1959, you, being directors of Shanahan's Stamp Auctions Limited, did conspire, combine, confederate and agree to cheat and defraud the public in that you did advertise in the public press, auctions of stamps being held from time to time during the said period by the said company at premises in Dun Laoghaire, and did, thereby, invite the public to entrust money for investment in Shanahan's Stamp Auctions Limited for the purchase and sale of stamps at those auctions, by pretending that the auctions were honestly conducted; whereas, you knew in fact, that the moneys being invested were grouped by you into syndicates, and that dividends were being paid by Shanahan's Stamp Auctions Limited on moneys invested by the public, without reference to the prices at which stamps were sold, and that you decided what dividends should be paid after each auction was held, and for that purpose, you created fictitious purchasers and also the prices at which stamps were alleged to have been sold on behalf of the various syndicates; and that you charged commission and paid dividends to the investors in those syndicates, and for the purpose of paying those dividends, you used moneys entrusted to

146

Shanahan's Stamp Auctions Limited by members of the public who were not members of the syndicates concerned.

THE SINGERS' COUNSEL, Seán Hooper, dismissed any possibility of Irma Singer being involved in fraud. All she had done was the routine marking of catalogues, he said. Regarding Paul Singer, he held that the State had failed to specify any investor who had lost money nor did it justify its claim that £750,000 had left the country or that £1,000,000 was missing. Paying one investor with another's money was not proven either, he held. He denied illegality on his client's part and reminded the court that the stamps held securely in bank vaults had increased in value by 11% since their seizure by the State.

Ulick O'Connor defended his client with vigour, pointing out that he knew nothing about stamp values and he accepted Singer's word. The prosecution did not prove that Arthur Desmond knew that the company was operating fraudulently, as alleged.

Mr O'Connor's submission had the effect of arousing public sympathy for the Shanahans. It also sowed the seed of suggestion that there was a split in the Singer/Shanahan camp.

For Great War veteran Jerome Shanahan, William Fanning painted a picture of a non-executive, handyman who met visiting buyers, attended to customs duties and helped out generally. Although described as chairman of the company, he signed neither cheques nor the annual report (his name did appear as Chairman in the 1958 Annual Report published in *The Irish Times* and shown on page 139).

When Walter Carroll summed up, his speech further suggested, perhaps unintentionally, a Shanahan-Singer rift. It also derided Singer by quoting a letter from one of the last Shanahan catalogues. This read:

Dear Mr Burrus,

You might be interested to learn that I got safely back after a pleasant flight from Geneva, via London. I was received at Dublin airport to my great surprise by a crowd of about 200-

300 people, staff, investors, philatelists and other friends, who had heard about my Burrus transactions and who gave me an almost regal welcome, singing *For He's a Jolly Good Fellow*, Irish songs, clapping their hands, cheering me, and so on. This never happened to a philatelist before.

Let me thank you, dear Mr Burrus, for Ireland, for Shanahan's Stamp Auctions Limited, and for myself.

With great devotion,
Paul Singer

Carroll added: 'You can approach Singer and his culpability by taking into consideration the bilge he has written in that letter.' Then he reiterated Singer's modus operandi, ending with an assertion that Singer handled his investors' money more or less as he pleased and that the other three directors knew the firm's operations were not genuine.

On the sixty-third day of the hearing, 23 January 1960, District Justice O'Flynn discharged Jerome Shanahan and sent his son and the two Singers for trial on warrants 'to the next sitting of the Circuit Criminal Court'. That phrase was common enough parlance, but the State did not reckon with the clever Paul Singer, who would use two of its words to his advantage in a manner that would rock the institutions of the State and infuriate its citizens.

ARTHUR DESMOND SHANAHAN and Irma Singer availed of bail. In Mountjoy Prison, Paul Singer put his legal knowledge to good use. As he studied tomes to further his own case, he also helped fellow-prisoners and was credited with obtaining some releases from custody. After about nine weeks, he demanded and received a hearing in the Dublin District Criminal Court. He complained to the Judge about the delay in sending him for trial and asked for his release from Mountjoy. The Judge refused. Little did the honourable gentleman know that a refusal was exactly what Singer wanted.

On 10 April, Singer wrote to the Attorney General stating that he had not yet been brought to trial and was therefore in unlawful custody. All he received was an acknowledgement of his letter. There was no reply from the prison governor to a similar petition. A few more weeks passed and, on 20 April, before Justice Budd in the High Court, Singer sought a conditional order under Section 6 of the Habeas Corpus Act, directing the Governor of Mountjoy and the Attorney General to release him from custody.

Singer played his trump card, and explained how, in January, he was sent for trial to the *Next Sitting* of the Circuit Criminal Court. That Court had sat on two occasions since that pronouncement. Singer had not been arraigned or indicted nor did the State seek an adjournment on either occasion. There was argument about interpretation of Section 6, but Mr Justice Budd granted the conditional order of habeas corpus. Singer was to remain in custody for six days, the time given to the Attorney General and Governor to show just cause why the order should not be made absolute.

His own legal study and skill had gained Singer this significant advantage. For his final push, he engaged Seán MacBride.

MacBride had been a staunch defender of Republicans charged under the Treason, Offences against the State and Emergency Powers Acts. The founder of the Clann na Poblachta Party, he had served as Minister for External Affairs in the 1948-1951 inter-party government. He was recognised as a leading constitutional and defence lawyer. For the Singer case, MacBride's junior counsel was Noel Hartnett, who was also Irma Singer's counsel.

On 28 April, Paul Singer, Irma Singer and Arthur Desmond Shanahan appeared before Judge Conroy in the Circuit Criminal Court. Ulick O'Connor pleaded illegality of the proceedings in view of the pending High Court ruling on Singer's application. The Justice disagreed and Shanahan was arraigned, sent for trial and released on continuing bail. For Irma Singer, Mr Hartnett successfully sought an adjournment, because he had received copies of the indictment only on the previous day. For the Attorney General, Mr Niall McCarthy asked for an adjournment in Paul Singer's case. Commentators suggest that this indicated his faith in the failure of Singer's High Court venture the next day.

Mr Justice Cahir Davitt, President of the High Court, sat with Mr Justice Budd and Mr Justice Haugh. Seán MacBride held that Singer was being held in custody on an order that was then spent. Furthermore, because his commital order was bad in law, he was being held in custody unlawfully. MacBride's third contention was that holding Singer violated the Constitution and the elements of natural justice.

The State underlined the amount of money involved and the nature of the case which required taking depositions from up to 300 witnesses. There was no undue delay, it held. On the 'next sitting', plea in which Singer had placed so much faith, the ruling was that the term had no authority in law.

Singer lost the application and was billed for £800 costs. MacBride got leave to appeal to the Supreme Court and he did so.

The Supreme Court of five judges sat on 25 May and ordered Singer's release from prison. They agreed with the philatelic doctor's view on the 'next sitting'.

All hell broke loose in establishment circles. Superintendent Weymes, who had led the investigation, saw all his force's painstaking work in pinning down Singer being wasted unless there was hasty action.

In the Four Courts, Noel Hartnett was feverishly attending to securing a release order. In the Attorney General's office, a new warrant for Singer's arrest was being arranged. In both cases, speedy expedition was of the utmost importance. Each knew that even a few hours of freedom could give Singer a chance to escape from the jurisdiction. Singer packed his bags and left Mountjoy prison convinced that he was free. He walked a few steps from the door. Two detectives re-arrested him. A Garda car took him to the Bridewell where he faced new charges. The wording in these differed slightly, but significantly from the original ones. When he appeared before District Justice Farrell that evening, Singer protested, particularly at the high independent surety still being imposed for bail.

Next day, Irma Singer and Arthur Desmond Shanahan were arrested again, as well as the latter's wife, Diana. This new turn of events intrigued some and shocked others. Diana's arrest was so sudden and unexpected that she had to bring her youngest child into the courtroom with her. Ulick O'Connor protested vigorously on her behalf. He echoed the sentiments of many among the public who were following the case. Four days later Mr Ernest Wood joined Mr O'Connor in berating the Attorney General. Part of his speech went:

> So far, I have advised him to abstain from putting the Attorney General right where he has been guilty of clearly illegal practices. I had hoped that some kind of responsibility would have eventually arisen in the mind of the Attorney General, but it does not appear that this is going to happen. He appears, since Paul Singer exposed him, to have behaved with the irresponsibility of a child.
>
> Unless the Attorney General comes to his senses, and realises the elemental principle of justice that a man cannot stand charged in two courts with the same alleged offence at the one time, I will advise my client to bring proceedings which should not be necessary if the Attorney General realised his responsibility and behaved properly.
>
> I say this in an appeal to the Attorney General to realise that what he is doing in the case of Mr and Mrs Shanahan looks like the act of a forensic teddy-boy who is determined to destroy their family life. He must realise that while this case is pending, and it has been pending for a year now, Desmond Shanahan cannot take up any employment to earn his living while he faces the prospect of appearing day after day in this court, as he did on 63 occasions in the past twelve months. What has happened is a monstrous interference in the rights of the Shanahans and their family. The Attorney General ought to take steps at once to put his house in order – or I shall advise my client to do it for him.

Meanwhile the hearing was adjourned. Paul Singer was back in Mountjoy. His wife and the younger Shanahan couple were released on bail. In Dáil Éireann, the Attorney General was under severe attack. Deputies questioned his appointment, his private practice and his 'costly and clumsy handling' of the Singer case.

There was a hurried special sitting of the Central Criminal Court on 3 June. Sean MacBride had rushed back from Africa to defend Singer. There was complicated argument about whether his client was in court under duress or of his own free will. District Justice Walsh ruled that Singer was being illegally held in the court.

Once again Singer was free.

Once again there was commotion in the Attorney General's office.

Once again Singer walked a few free steps.

Once again he was arrested.

The Dublin wags were enjoying every minute of the Gilbertian situation.

Sewing machines having us all in stitches was the theme in their banter. Singers performed parodies on *Good Bye-ee* and *Don't Fence Me In* too:

> I get crams sticking stamps on the warders in Mountjoy,
>   Don't Fence Me In!
> Let me stride from inside, just a hundred yards, my boy,
>   Don't Fence Me In!

When the Court resumed the same day, Noel Hartnett and Justice Walsh played a cat-and-mouse game, with Hartnett refusing to plead on behalf of his client. Eventually there was stalemate and he left the court with Mrs Singer.

A.D. Shanahan's counsel, Ernest Wood, sought trial as soon as possible. Later in the day, with Justice Farrell presiding, the new charges against Arthur Desmond were struck out and he was released on continuing bail. Seán MacBride, having successfully saved Singer from paying costs, launched an attack on the State's bungling of the whole case. Mr Hartnett joined in and Justice Farrell adjourned the case for a week.

It was a week of parliamentary recrimination. The Dáil Debates Records for 1 June note the oral answers concerning 'State *vs* Singer':

Mr Ryan [Dublin: South West, Fine Gael] asked the Taoiseach [Mr Seán Lemass, Dublin: South Central, Fianna Fáil] whether in view of the failure of the Attorney General to bring to trial Paul Singer who was returned for trial in the Dublin Metropolitan District Court on 22 January last and of the fact that the same person was held in unlawful custody since 8 April last, he will in accordance with Article 30, section 5, subsection 2 of the Constitution request the resignation of the Attorney General.

The Taoiseach: The answer is in the negative.

I may add that I do not accept the Deputy's allegation that there has been a failure on the part of the Attorney General in respect of this matter.

Mr Dillon [Cavan Monaghan, Fine Gael]: Is the Taoiseach aware that there is a great deal of public uneasiness as to whether there has been a due and proper prosecution of the matters involved in this question and does the Taoiseach not think that, for the reassurance of the public, it would be right for him, on a suitable occasion, to make a considered statement on the whole proceedings in this connection?

The Taoiseach: The question at issue was whether the next sitting of the Circuit Criminal Court to which the accused was returned for trial meant a sitting during the current Hilary term of the Court or during the next following Easter term. Up to the time of the recent decision of the Supreme Court these two words 'term' and 'sitting' were always construed as synonymous and it was considered that the hearing of the case during the Easter term would comply fully with the provisions of the law. That point was contested. The matter was considered by three judges of the High Court who held unanimously that the previous view of the law was correct, that the case could properly come before the Circuit Criminal Court during the Easter term. On appeal to the Supreme Court, that Court held, by a majority of three to two, the contrary view. It will be seen therefore that of the eight superior court judges who considered this matter, five of them, including the Chief Justice and the President of the High Court, agreed with the view of the Attorney General and with the legality of the practice which was established over many years, and three disagreed. The fact that the three judges who disagreed constituted a majority of the Supreme Court has of course settled now what is the correct interpretation of the law.

Mr Dillon: I know the Taoiseach will agree with me that the last thing any of us wish to do is to conduct this trial in Dáil Éireann but I trust he does appreciate that there is very considerable anxiety, (1) about the apparent extravagant expenditure of public money and (2) about the interminable proceedings which appear to have resulted in a failure to bring the matter to trial and issue, which in the interests of all should be done with the least possible delay.

The Taoiseach: I should point out, it was not argued by Counsel representing the accused that there was any undue delay in the case and indeed there appears to have been agreement between prosecution and defence that the case could not have been heard earlier.

Mr Dillon: I am sure both the Taoiseach and I desire to avoid any attempt to try this case here but the interests of the accused and of the public have to be considered in a matter of this kind. Our concern here as the Legislature certainly should be to see that both are properly protected. There is grave general uneasiness about the interminable delays that have taken place in connection with the proceedings in this matter and, both from the point of view of the public and from the point of view of the person charged, I trust the Taoiseach will bear that in mind and exhort the Attorney General to see this issue is brought to trial at the earliest possible moment and decided upon.

The Taoiseach: The Deputy will appreciate it is not open to us to criticise the proceedings of the courts. In this case the practice followed by the law officers of the Government was identical with that which has been operated here for very many years and, while I do not pretend to understand fully the reasons for the Supreme Court decision, we have to accept their decision as involving a change of that practice in the future unless we should decide to change the law.

Mr Ryan: Is the Taoiseach aware that he has advanced arguments here which were not advanced in either the

High Court or the Supreme Court by the Attorney General or on behalf of the Attorney General?

The Taoiseach: I am not aware I have advanced any arguments at all.

Mr Ryan: Is he not aware that at the time the person concerned was returned for trial there was a Circuit Court sitting and that the simple translation or understanding of the word 'next' is the next sitting –

An Ceann Comhairle: It is not within our jurisdiction to interpret.

The Taoiseach: That is the point that was argued, but I say in that connection that of the eight judges who considered this matter, five held the contrary view.

ON 7 JUNE Seán MacBride, Noel Hartnett and Ernest Wood again dwelt on the confusion brought about by the State. Niall McCarthy countered for the Attorney General. District Justice Farrell sent the four for trial.

Singer's success with a technicality changed the nature of court hearings. Lengthy procedures demanded by law had often been dispensed with to the relief of both parties in a case. In the remainder of the Paul Singer case, however, every effort was made to present everything with meticulous correctitude.

Arthur Desmond Shanahan's trial opened on 27 June 1960. The evidence was more or less as before, but this time Jerome Shanahan testified in his son's defence. Jerome's tragic circumstances tugged at the nation's heartstrings for he was by then working as a night watchman in England. He stated that he had even lost his own investment in stamps. Arthur Desmond said, in evidence, that Singer worked his staff so hard that he (Arthur) had to give up all recreation and even bring his wife into the firm in order to save their marriage. As staff and experts were cross-examined, their evidence was suggesting more and more that Singer led the Shanahans and others a merry skip if not a dance. If the jury was not convinced, Mr Ernest Wood, in his summing up, clearly laid the blame at Singer's feet.

In the Dáil on 20 July, Dr Noel Browne, the Independent deputy for Dublin South-East, who, in 1957 had formed the National Progressive Democratic Party, asked about detailed expenses to the State arising out of the case. Oscar Traynor, Minister for Justice, answered, giving the figure as £5,500 to date.

Dr Browne: Could I ask the Minister if there is any way in which the public can be indemnified against this costly blundering by this part-time Attorney General in his mishandling of the court cases in this way?

Dr Browne also asked if the Minister agreed that such indemnification was necessary if this was going to continue and if the Attorney General was not going to be asked to resign. The Taoiseach, Seán Lemass, said, 'The Deputy is always very zealous when he is attacking somebody who is not here to defend himself. That is typical of the Deputy.'

Mr Justice McLoughlin took a full working day to sum up on 21 July. The jury deliberated for almost as long. They found Shanahan guilty on 16 of the 21 counts, but reckoned that he had been unduly influenced and recommended leniency. He was sentenced to 15 months' imprisonment.

Paul Singer was still contesting the Attorney General's right to hear new charges against him. He was granted a temporary order to that effect on 4 July and on the same day, District Justice Farrell ruled that he could not go ahead with the case against Irma Singer and Diana Shanahan because, in his own words, the case was in a mess.

More fresh charges were made against Singer on 10 July. More wrangling took place, with Singer still seeking a release order of habeas corpus. The State's team was now headed by Richard McGonigal. He and MacBride fell to a type of bargaining, both knowing that the country and the government were now out to get Singer.

It would be an understatement to say that a merry-go-round of appearances and hearings took place thereafter. Involved and heated argument resulted, finally, in Singer being returned for trial on 17 October. There still was a

Supreme Court Appeal to be heard. During their normal vacation period, five Judges sat on 4 August. One of them, Mr Justice Lavery, had ruled in favour of Singer at the first hearing. This time, he and the other four were unanimous. Singer would not go free. He would stand trial. Worse for the learned doctor – costs were awarded to the Attorney General.

The trial that so many people wanted got under way in Green Street on 17 October 1960. Singer and his wife were arraigned. Irma's previous advocate, Noel Hartnett had died and, because of that, Desmond Bell successfully sought an adjournment in her case. Singer conducted his own defence. He began by claiming that a fair trial was impossible because of the amount of publicity the case had got. Witnesses gave evidence that by then was familiar to the many whose interest in the 'Singer Affair' had grown every day. The case had now been in the public arena for 19 months. Staff members of Shanahans gave laborious details of transactions. Eleven days into the trial a Mr Paul Shanahan, William Street, Listowel, Co. Kerry, an agent for Shanahan's Stamp Auctions Ltd., said his commission was 9d in £1. Singer asked him how much he earned from January 1958. Shanahan replied, 'Roughly between £4,000 and £5,000'.

On 7 November, Mr Noel Gough, chartered accountant, gave evidence. He said that during the five-month period from January to May 1959, a total of £1,927,206 was invested in Shanahan's Stamp Auctions Ltd. He said after the burglary period in May 1959, investments practically stopped and only a trickle of money was coming in.

Gough helped to make an analysis of the accounts of Shanahan's Stamp Auctions for the Attorney General. The books, he said, showed that in one sale, on 29 November 1958, there were 1,266 investors, who had invested a total of £174,397. The value of stamps allocated to the sale was £42,420. The amount realised for these stamps was £52,319. The total repayment was £215,083. Commission for the company was £21,295 leaving a net payment to the syndicate in the sale of £193,787. The profit paid to investors was £19,390.

In respect of a sale due to be held on 9 May 1959, Mr Gough said that there were 1,971 investors with a total investment of £255,503. A circular from the company said, to be fair to everyone, the company had decided to pay 25/6d for every £1 to all investors, less commission. This, the circular stated, was slightly higher than the average gain per four-month period for 1958. He said the total sum required to pay this 25/6d in the £1 would be £293,189. Two hundred and eight of 1,971 investors received a total of £25,826.

Hugh Finlay, cashier at Shanahan's, told the court on 7 November that, after the buying of the Burrus collection he went to Dublin Airport because Singer telephoned instructing him to do so. Singer asked him to contact the newspapers and represent himself as a person with no interest in Shanahan's and to say that, while at the airport, he heard people singing *For He's a Jolly Good Fellow*. Mr Finlay said he did that but he did not think there had been a word of publicity from any sources.

On 11 November Mr Gerard O'Brien, liquidator said that the assets of the company were:

Cash in hand: £2,671
Cash at National Bank College Green: £5,930

Subsequently, £51,395 was received from a Swiss bank; £30,815 from a bank in Toronto; £1,104 from a bank in New Zealand; £4,942 from a bank in New York.

The money in the Swiss and Canadian banks was in the names of Singer/Dr Paul and/or Irma; the money in the New York bank was in the name of Shanahan's Stamp Auctions Ltd. A total of £86,426 had been recovered from foreign banks and there was £18,479 owing to the company for stamps sold, and not paid for.

The total of outstanding debts to the company was £32,000. Furniture and fittings sold realised £6,058 and sale of philatelic literature realised £1,084. Value of claims against the company which had been passed was £1,840,000.

Some public commentators had decided that Singer had a hand in the stamp robbery at Shanahan's. They got their answer during the trial when Swiss police recovered £290,000 worth of them. The *Irish Independent* reported:

GENEVA STAMPS ARREST
EXTRADITION OF COUPLE MAY BE SOUGHT

The Government is considering whether to ask the government of Switzerland to hand over a former employee of Shanahan's Stamps Auctions Ltd., Dun Laoghaire, and his wife ... Two Irish police officers flew to Geneva on Sunday and requested Interpol to interview the couple who were arrested over a week ago in connection with trading and stamps alleged to have been stolen from Shanahan's premises in May of last year. The police officers, Detective Superintendent T. Culhane and Detective Inspector Patrick Kenny, yesterday interviewed the couple in Geneva and later in the day the authorities in Dublin considered sending a request to the Swiss authorities for the return of the couple to this country. The difficulty facing the government is that it has no extradition treaty with Switzerland and legal moves to prevent the couple being handed over to the Irish police are anticipated. The Irish police officers, it is stated, may return to Dublin tomorrow. The man who was interviewed in Geneva is a Greek, Apostoles Tatsopoulos.

The Greek was a Shanahan staff member, a 'describer' of stamps. He was imprisoned as a result. On 15 November Singer said, 'I know it has been suggested that [the robbery] was all a fake but fortunately for me ... £290,000 worth of stamps were recovered and two people, one of them a prosecution witness, were arrested in a foreign country. It would have been an outrage of justice if you had allowed even a fleeting suspicion to enter your minds that there had

159

been no burglary or that I had been connected with it. However, a substantial portion of the prosecution evidence related to the burglary – it is left to you as an "unsolved mystery" – the prosecution hoping that in tendering this evidence they would create at least suspicions in your minds. Now gentlemen, the "mystery" has been at least partially solved.'

On 18 November, Singer referred to this again and said, 'If things go as they are planned, the investors will get very little in spite of the recovery of a large portion of the stolen stamps. The liquidator, Mr O'Brien, an efficient, conscientious accountant, is not a philatelist. I am embarrassed to say this but I do not think there is anyone in Ireland more qualified than I (sic) to advise him. To him, a stamp is just something you stick on a letter.'

Although he did not testify, Singer spoke for four days. He told the jury that he had been blackened and that, in his case, the 'innocent until proven guilty rule of law' had been reversed. He claimed that he kept the Ten Commandments and paid his staff well. Only the burglary murdered 'the sputnik of philately' that he had made Shanahan's Stamp Auctions. Diana Shanahan, he claimed, was a brilliant woman with a passion for figures. Even when she was having babies, she had arranged for an adding machine to be brought to her maternity hospital room. 'She was a queen bee,' Singer said. Her husband, he alleged, was weak 'and often like putty in the hands of his attractive but very hysterical wife'. Cleverly, he pointed out that the Shanahans had three votes to the Singers' two and that he himself was little more than an agent for the firm. He accused State witnesses of coming to warped conclusions.

Summing up, Mr Justice Haugh praised Superintendent Weymes and his team of Gardaí and detectives. He disputed Singer's allegation that his being a Jew mitigated against a fair trial. Haugh's main point was a simple one and was really asking where the money that had been lodged abroad had gone?

Before they retired at 7.15 p.m. Mr Justice Haugh directed the jury to return a verdict of 'not guilty' on two counts

160

because of what he called 'overlapping'. These counts, he said, were dealt with in greater detail in two other charges.

IT WAS MONDAY 21 November 1960. After an hour and 20 minutes, the jury found Paul Singer guilty on 19 charges of fraud, conspiracy and fraudulent conversion of '£796,514.6s 2d to the use and benefit of Shanahan's Stamp Auctions Ltd. being the amount to which, as alleged, it appeared the company was indebted to investors at the date of liquidation'.

Mr Justice Haugh did not pass sentence. He gave Singer a week to deliberate. The *Irish Independent* began its story the next day:

> Head erect, his hands clutching the dockrail of the Green Street Courthouse, Dr Paul Singer looked towards the jury in the Central Criminal Court, Dublin, and showed no emotion as he heard their verdict, 'Guilty on all counts, My Lord'. Singer looked straight at Mr Justice Haugh as he heard him tell the jury, 'I fully agree with your verdict, gentlemen, but Singer must wait another week before he knows what sentence will be passed'. The Judge told him, 'I do not intend to propose sentence this evening in the present atmosphere of emotion and excitement. I propose to postpone sentence for one week to give you a chance to think matters over. It will be my duty, however, to impose a very heavy sentence.' Mr Justice Haugh said he would give Singer the week to make up his mind if he would disclose to the liquidator where and when large sums of money were lodged. 'That money is still somewhere ... either in credit or in stamps,' he said.

So ended the longest criminal trial in the history of the State. It had lasted 25 days, and millions of words had been written and spoken. The previous longest trial was that of Arthur Desmond Shanahan, fellow director and former

161

secretary. In Singer's case there were 1,895 exhibits representing some 5,000 documents and 10,000 pages.

The public waited. The week passed. Singer divulged nothing. The deficiency, he insisted, was based on the valuation of one witness, Mr Lowe. Mr Justice Haugh then asked Singer if he had anything to say. He replied: 'I have been thinking very carefully about what Your Lordship said last Monday night and I wish to reiterate here and now that all the money entrusted to me for the purchase of stamps for investors was, in fact, so used by me except for 83,000 Canadian Dollars which I repatriated to the National Bank, College Green, Dublin. The so-called deficiency arises solely from the differences in evaluations given by Mr Robson Lowe and those which the company offered for the stamps in Dun Laoghaire.'

Singer added that, shortly before May 1959, on instructions from the liquidator, he had closed his accounts in Zurich, and the First City Bank of Nova Scotia, and had remitted the outstanding credit balances to the liquidator. 'There are no hidden monies anywhere,' he said, 'and all the money entrusted to me is fully accounted for by stamp purchases and for the investors. I wish to confirm that I am most anxious to help the liquidator to as much money as possible for distribution to the investors and I will always do anything in my power that he may reasonably ask of me. This is my solemn promise.'

Singer asked Haugh to take into consideration that he had spent 16 months in Mountjoy awaiting trial, and despite the fact that he had enjoyed privileges while on remand that this was the equivalent of a two-year sentence with remission. He added that Arthur Desmond Shanahan had been sentenced to 15 months on the same charges. 'Even if I were released today,' he added, 'I would still have served a 50% longer sentence than he, and, under the circumstances, a much greater mental strain and torture. There is a principle of equality of treatment in Irish law and I hope Your Lordship will apply this in the interest of fair play, justice and humanity.'

The Judge spoke again, at length. The Incorporated Council of Law Reporting in Ireland records the official outcome thus:

Paul Singer, was found guilty at the Central Criminal Court on 21 November, 1960, on one charge of conspiracy (count 3), 16 charges of fraudulent conversion (counts 4 to 19) and 2 charges of obtaining money by false pretences (counts 20 and 21), and on the 28 November, 1960, he was sentenced by the presiding Judge, Mr Justice Haugh, to 15 years' penal servitude in all, as fol-lows: on counts 5 to 19, 7 years' penal servitude concurrent on each count; counts 20 and 21, 5 years' penal servitude concurrent on each count, concurrent with the preceding sentence; count 3, 3 years' penal servitude, also concurrent with the preceding sentence; count 4, on completion of the 7 years' penal servitude already imposed, another 7 years' penal servitude. On two charges of conspiracy (counts 1 and 2) the applicant was, by direction of the trial judge, found not guilty.

The *Irish Independent* put the sentence at one year less:

Dr Paul Singer, 49 year old former Managing Director of Shanahan's Stamp Auctions Ltd., Dun Laoghaire, looked quite unmoved as he stood, one hand on his hip, the other clutching the dock rail of the Central Criminal Court, Dublin, yesterday and listened to Mr Justice Haugh sentence him to a total of fourteen years' penal servitude. A crowded, hushed court earlier heard the Judge tell Singer that his treatment of the public who invested money, 'Maybe their entire savings' in the company, was 'deliberately ruthless and merciless in the extreme'. The Judge believed that it was still well within Singer's power to atone and partly undo the ruin he had already caused. The Justice also said 'The evidence has satisfied me that you were the person behind the company's many fraudulent activities'. Mr Justice Haugh refused Singer's application to appeal which had been based on seventeen grounds.

One startling revelation concerned the foreman of the jury. Singer claimed that he was a chartered accountant employed by Messrs Craig Gardner and Company, the firm in which Gerard O'Brien, the Shanahan liquidator, was a senior partner. He was also an investor in Shanahan's Stamp Auctions and a claimant against the company in the liquidation, in respect of his investment.

In February 1961, after another long period of sittings, informations were refused against Diana Shanahan. Yet one year later she was summoned to stand trial. Seán MacBride fought the decision and won. She was free. Not so, said the Supreme Court.

THE COURT OF Criminal Appeal sat at the Four Courts on 11 April 1961. Mr Justices Walsh, Murnaghan and O'Dalaigh pitted their wits against Singer, who again asserted that no investor had ever lost money. Since Arthur Desmond Shanahan had been acquitted of his conspiracy charge, the same should apply to him. He derided the trial Judge's summing up and in the manner in which he had passed sentence. Furthermore, he was the judge taking liquidation proceedings in the High Court and Singer claimed that he used his trial 'to further the ends of the liquidation proceedings'.

Once again, Paul Singer succeeded. A re-trial was ordered; his 14 year sentence was cancelled. The judges ruled that there had been faulty overlapping in the original charges and that Singer should be tried on just nine charges: Counts 5, 12, 13, 14, 15, 16, 17, 18 and 19. Count 4, charging Singer with the fraudulent conversion of £796, 514.6s.2d, would not be re-tried. The total fraudulent conversion figure in the charges being re-tried totalled only £1,800.

Full of confidence now, Singer pointed out that his bail figure should be reduced. It was – to a personal surety of £3,000 and an independent surety of the same amount. On 7 July, Singer succeeded in having the independent surety decreased to £1,500. He sought permission from Mr Justice Teevan to go abroad for a personal reason. The Judge refused. Again Singer sought his £780.00 that the Gardaí had seized from his home over two years previously. He got it.

A Dun Laoghaire publican, Hugh Larkin signed the bail bond after District Justice Farrell warned Singer not to leave the State. With over two years in jail behind him, flashes of the old Dr Singer appeared as he posed for the press photographers. Then it was off to a modest flat in Dun Laoghaire with Irma, who still had not been tried.

While Singer awaited his re-trial, the liquidator of Shanahan's Stamp Auctions made an attempt to have him testify in court. Seán MacBride successfully pleaded that this would prejudice the re-trial. Five Supreme Court judges agreed.

The re-trial lasted a record 47 days. Singer had used his waiting period of three months well. Seán MacBride and Gerard Charleton added a young Paul Callan to their defence team. The team went over familiar ground. Mr Justice Walsh delivered a long address. This ended with his saying that the case against Singer could not be proven either affirmatively or negatively. 'The prosecution have to prove it affirmatively – and it is not for the accused to prove his innocence. As the case stands, the prosecution must fail.' He instructed the jury to record a verdict of not guilty.

Seamus Brady recorded Singer's days in court at 262 and quoted legal experts as saying that the cost to the state £250,000. Singer must have felt four times that as he walked from the courtroom to a robing room where a party was arranged. He signed autographs for jury members, spoke of his hardships and financial problems and of going to visit his mother in Canada. He and Irma then took a taxi to their flat. The next morning they had vanished.

POSTSCRIPT

Was Singer afraid to face the bankruptcy court? He sent a cable saying that he would like to attend, but that his mother was unwell. The liquidator cabled the address he had supplied but he was unknown there. Hired private detectives could not find him. Was he still laughing at the establishment?

Would he write the book he promised during the party following his aquittal?

None has emerged.

Diana Shanahan's case was listed for December 1962. By that time she had left Ireland with her husband, who had served his sentence, the only person in the Shanahan's Stamp Auctions affair to do so.

Meanwhile, on 27 March 1962, Dr Ryan (T.D., Wexford, Fianna Fáil), Minister for Finance, gave Mr Sweetman (Kildare, Fine Gael) details of the cost to the State of Singer's two habeas corpus actions, his appeals and his retrial. A sum of £576.10.6d. had been paid in respect of the first High Court action. Bills for the second had been taxed at £101.7.4d. For the Court of Criminal Appeal, the amount taxed was £219.18.0d. Dr Ryan would not give details of amounts paid to Counsel for the Attorney General but said that £24,410 had been paid from the Law Charges Vote.

Two days later, on 29 March 1962, there was a witty exchange in the Dáil. William Norton (Kildare, Labour) asked C.J. Haughey (Dublin: North East, Fianna Fáil), Minister for Justice, 'whether the recent decision of the courts in the Singer case means the complete acquittal of Mr Singer; if not, whether any further charges are to be preferred against him; and if so, how many charges; and when they will be preferred'.

Mr Haughey: Mr Singer has been acquitted on all charges brought against him.
Mr Norton: The legal machine has done this gentleman proudly. It could not happen in a banana republic.
Mr Haughey: I have never been in a banana republic.
Mr Norton: Mr Singer, with all our people's money in his pocket, is in one at the moment and enjoying himself to his heart's content.

Holidaymakers have reported sightings of the doctor from time to time. Newspapers have published photographs of a slimmer, clean-shaven look-alike – in Marbella, in Munich, in Canada.

Early in 1963 the cases against Diana Shanahan and Irma Singer were dropped. A *nolle prosequi* was entered. The State was unwilling to continue. Mrs Singer's father got his bail money back – with interest!

One thing resulted from the fiasco: after the Singer case, the State became extremely careful about expediting arraignment as soon as possible after sending an accused for trial.

To this day, Ulick O'Connor has not altered his views on the Singer case. He says: 'I think the Attorney General should never have brought the case, because the stamps would have appreciated in value. As it was, investors recouped 50%. Without five years of legal expenses, their losses would have been minimal, if there were any. I believe Shanahan's Stamp Auctions Ltd. was a legitimate operation. Paul Singer had acquired part of the Burrus collection. If he had exercised his option to purchase the remainder, he would have controlled the stamp world. Therefore, I believe that Singer's enemies in that same stamp world planned the robbery to destroy him.'

THE ROSE TATTOO AFFAIR

The late Alan Simpson was born in Dublin in 1920. He received his education in Belfast and Trinity College, Dublin. Qualifying as an engineer, he joined the army and served during the World War II. After The Emergency he worked with the Edwards-MacLiammoir company for a while, but re-joined the Corps of Engineers and rose to the rank of Captain. While in the army, he married Carolyn Swift and the couple founded the tiny Pike Theatre in a garage and roofed yard at Herbert Lane, Dublin. It opened in September 1953. Late night 'Follies' were a feature of the programme, but the forward-thinking company also staged Beckett and Behan during its first four years in business.

For the first Dublin Theatre Festival in May 1957, the Pike decided to produce *The Rose Tattoo*, a play by the American playwright, Tennessee Williams. This work concerns a Sicilian widow in New Orleans, Serafina Delle Rosa. While driving for the mob, her husband is killed when his truck crashes. Serafina enshrines his ashes in her home. Extraordinarily religious, yet highly sexed, she locks up her daughter, Rosa, to protect her morals. On the verge of a nervous breakdown, the arrival of another truck-driver, Alvaro Mangiacavallo, rescues her. He has designs on Serafina. During one scene he pulls his hands from his pocket and, unknown to himself, lets something fall on the floor. Serafina sees it and is furious. She screams and abuses him about the dreadful object he has dropped, then sends the man off to his lorry. The word 'contraceptive' is not mentioned, but little is left to the imagination. Certainly not to some Irish imaginations!

Festival Director, Brendan Smith, admitted to receiving a protest letter from a group called 'The League of Decency' who objected to the play's inclusion in the Festival programme, he said, because it 'advocated the use of birth control by unnatural means'. Smith contacted Simpson.

Alan was the son of a Church of Ireland clergyman, yet he consulted with a devout Roman Catholic member of the cast who then went to Smith and cited cases when he had turned down parts because of their moral or religious shortcomings. He assured him that he had no scruples about *The Rose Tattoo*. Smith, after consultation with Simpson, marked the letter 'Read' and carried on with planning the Festival.

The play opened in the Pike to rave notices. In *The Sunday Times*, Harold Hobson hinted that Herbert Lane was on its way to becoming as distinguished a thoroughfare as Abbey Street or Cavendish Row, locations of the Abbey and Gate respectively. In the *Evening Press*, the former critic of the *Catholic Standard*, Gabriel Fallon, praised the play: '[It] gives rise to the possibility that the Irish (deep down at all events) have much in common with the Sicilians. Or is it that Mr Williams has unexpectedly touched universality in this play? Go and see it. It will be well worth your while.'

Simpson had contrived the questionable scene 'in such a way that any persons not sophisticated enough to appreciate the implications of the situation would remain in ignorance as to what was supposed to have taken place. 'Those Catholics who understood would, I felt, appreciate the implied compliment to the Faith.' Simpson said, 'That I was largely successful in my attempt to handle these more delicate matters without offence is borne out by Mr Hobson's description of the direction as being of "outstanding discrimination".'

Fifteen minutes before the second performance, a police inspector called to the Pike and asked to see Mr Simpson. He was busy upstairs negotiating a proposed transfer of the production to the Gate Theatre, but reluctantly he came down and met the inspector. He was told that it had been brought to the attention of the authorities, that the Tennessee Williams play contained 'objectionable passages'. Reading from a prepared script, the Inspector instructed that the imminent performance should be cancelled. Simpson said he would have to consult with his solicitor. Before doing so, however, he told his wife to take up the curtain.

Con Lehane, a former Clann na Poblachta T.D., had helped Simpson previously. Con was associated with the Republican movement and was friendly with Seán MacBride. This solicitor arrived at Herbert Lane and asked to see the document that had been read to Simpson. The inspector refused, but he agreed to read it aloud. Lehane jotted down what he heard. There were no further developments that night but next day, Lehane wrote to the Deputy Commissioner of the Garda Síochána who had originated the document, requesting that the 'offensive passages' be stipulated.

Meanwhile, Simpson tried to keep the affair quiet. He even indicated some willingness to make certain cuts in order to save the Festival committee embarrassment. The Lord Mayor, Robert Briscoe, was chairman of the Dublin Tóstal Council, under whose patronage the Theatre Festival was held. Simpson was shocked to receive no support from Briscoe, but an admonishment for daring to present such a play – a play, Simpson claimed, that Briscoe had not seen. Erskine Childers, Fianna Fáil Minister for Lands, another Festival patron, also disapproved. Many years later, Carolyn Swift declared in *Stage By Stage* (Dublin, 1985):

> One friend [who later became] an ambassador, feeling as we did that a mistake must have been made and incredulous at our reports, went away to make enquiries, convinced he had only to drop a word in the right quarters for all to be fixed. He came back to us much shaken.
>
> 'I can only tell you it comes from the very top,' he said. 'Dev himself [Eamonn de Valera, Taoiseach, Fianna Fáil] wants action taken against you.'

Because the play was to transfer to the Gate the following week, Simpson informed Lord Longford, the theatre's producer, of the difficulties. Again he received no support. Longford placed cancellation notices in the newspapers and now the cat was well and truly out of the bag. Simpson drafted a press release in an apt location – the monkey-house at the Dublin Zoo, where he had taken his daughter for her birthday.

He went to Lehane to clear the document with him. While there, a note arrived from the Garda Deputy Commissioner stating that the whole matter was 'being dealt with by the proper authorities according to law'. Simpson rushed his hot news to the gentlemen of the press, who devoured it.

Squad cars were waiting at Herbert Lane that evening, their occupants ready to accost Simpson, but a friendly warning gave him the chance to reach the theatre without passing them.

When they realised that Simpson had given them the slip, the Garda Síochána sent for him, but he refused to come to the top of the lane. So they converged on the tiny theatre and, after a minor scuffle, arrested him. Simpson's version of the fracas suggests that four burly plain-clothes detectives insisted on interviewing him in the tiny box-office. He demurred. Two of them dragged him in forcibly, at the same time pushing Carolyn Swift roughly into the lane and slamming the door on the house-manager's wrist. At the Bridewell, they charged him with 'presenting for gain an indecent and profane performance' (later, the word 'profane' was replaced by 'indecent'). They refused him bail, and placed him in a cell.

Con Lehane visited him and was not optimistic, because the arrest had been made on a summary warrant, the type normally reserved for armed criminals and dangerous IRA members. Simpson spent a most uncomfortable night in the cell. He describes the experience in his book, *Beckett and Behan and a Theatre in Dublin* (London, 1962): '... I was made to turn out my pockets, and all sharp instruments such as my nail clippers, keys and cigarette lighter were removed from me ... A rather surly warder obtained a meal for me, which I consumed without relish. Later he was replaced by a more genial character, who inquired with sincere sympathy if it were naked women I was in for. When I told him it wasn't, he sadly remarked that "they" were "very funny in this country about them things". He then gave practical vent to his sympathy by obtaining me a miniature bottle of Irish whiskey, "a Baby Power".'

As he sipped this, Simpson pondered on the possible outcome of all this. He could receive up to two years' imprisonment. That, or even a nominal sentence, would incur automatic discharge from the army, with consequent loss of pension rights.

Meanwhile, at Simpson's request, Lehane conveyed a message to the Pike to have Alan replaced in the Late Night Revue. Charlie Roberts was to take his place so Carolyn Swift seized the glorious opportunity, went before the audience and announced that 'owing to the unavoidable arrest of Mr Alan Simpson', Mr Charles Roberts would play his roles in the performance. After laughter and applause, she explained everything that had happened.

Next morning Lehane told Simpson that if he undertook to take off the play, the matter would be dropped. If he refused, the State would oppose the granting of bail and he could spend weeks in custody before a trial. Simpson refused.

The courtroom was packed with cast and friends as the proceedings took place and the hearing was fixed for July 1957. The State did indeed oppose bail – vigorously. Holy Ireland had to be protected from this pariah in its midst, a man who advocated lewdness, and indecency. His release from custody would mean exposing the full cast to similar charges, it was implied. Luckily for the accused, the District Justice was a keen amateur actor. He granted bail, £50 from Simpson and £50 from an independent surety. An army legal officer, Seamus Heron, provided the independent surety. Outside the courtroom, Simpson received an ovation that many of his actor colleagues would have envied. Beyond his own circle, however, holy Ireland began to cast its verdict – the Ireland that turned a blind eye to wife-beating; the Ireland that regarded as a 'hard man' the fellow who got disgustingly drunk and excused all he did because of it; the Ireland that deemed it necessary to keep sex a suppressed subject. Róisín Dubh, the Rose Taboo!

172

There were rumours around Dublin that the cast had been arrested. They had indeed been threatened with prosecution but the play went ahead that night. Carolyn Swift had her own particular memory of events (and conveyed them in a letter to the author):

Alan Simpson had been charged in the District Court and, despite vigorous objections from the prosecution, freed on bail after an uncomfortable night in the Bridewell. I was standing in the wings, waiting to go on in the part of Rosa in place of Kate Binchy. She, unlike the rest of the cast, had been unable to defy the warning given to each and every one of us before the show that, if we set foot on the stage, we would be rendering ourselves liable to prosecution. Sobbing, she had been led away after her father had explained that since she was a minor, he was responsible for her actions and, himself being a judge, he could not very well defy the law, whatever his personal opinions.

I was 17 years older than Kate and quite unsuitable for the role of the fifteen year old schoolgirl. On a practical level, I was twice her size and there was no way of getting her dress to zip up the back. But there was no one else who could have learned the part in the time available whereas I, as assistant director, had been at every rehearsal and knew her every move and inflection. So there I was, with a white cardigan covering the open zip of her white graduation dress and scared out of my wits, not of the police lining the back of the auditorium, but of making vulgar what had been innocent, sensitive and beautiful. I kept praying that I would be arrested before I reached the love scene!

Kate's dress was suffocatingly tight but, even so, I suddenly became aware of an even greater strain on it. Looking down, I saw that the goat, who played an important part in the play and was also waiting for his entrance, was eating the very clothes off my back. As I heard the action on stage reaching a point only a few speeches before my cue, I began a wrestling match with the goat as I tugged my skirt back, inch by inch, out of his champing jaws.

No sooner had I won this battle than I was faced with another; that of competing on stage with the voice of Brendan Behan. With ... District Justice Donagh MacDonagh [who was a poet], he had come down to the theatre to demonstrate on our behalf. Spotting the goat, who was walked up and down in the lane outside between his entrances, he had launched, with typical and ready wit, into a spirited rendering of *The Peeler and the Goat*. This was clearly audible inside the theatre.

Simpson's army colleagues were there to support him. Brendan Behan, as Ms Swift confirmed, turned up and sang rebel songs. There was quite a 'hoolie' in Herbert Lane that night. Inside, two policemen who had failed to get seats for opening night, watched the play.

With no larger theatre to play in after the Pike, Simpson was forced to curtail the run there in order to save money. Perhaps saving the cast from arrest was a consideration too.

An English theatre magazine, *Encore*, set up a Defence Fund. Seán O'Casey, John Osborne, Wolf Mankowitz, John Gielgud, Harold Hobson, George Devine, Ben W. Levy and Peter Hall signed a letter seeking contributions. In Ireland, director Jim FitzGerald attempted to do the same. He failed to get any well-known people to sign, although some promised to contribute anonymously. An American appeal under the names of Derek Bentley, Padraic Colum, Denis Johnston, Frank O'Connor, Vivian Mercier, Eric Bentley, Kevin Sullivan and Edward Mulhare raised some money too.

Before the taking of depositions began, the play moved to the Royal Belfast Opera House. The police there described it as Sunday school fare. Dublin detectives involved in the case attended. The Dublin District Court hearing opened before District Justice Flynn on 4 July. In the main, evidence blackened Simpson and the Pike Theatre as purveyors of sordid plays. Yet one witness owned to having attended only two plays in his life. The Williams text used by the State in the proceedings was bought in Duffy's bookshop, stockists of Catholic and religious literature as well as play-scripts. Hugh Leonard covered the proceedings for a British magazine. Twenty-eight years later he recalled what had happened in his *Sunday Independent* column:

> In the dock, as it were, stood not only Mr Simpson, but a play, *The Rose Tattoo* by Tennessee Williams, and a detective-sergeant was attempting to sum up the plot.
> He had admitted to having been to the theatre only twice in the past 20 years. Nonetheless, no one was other than taken aback when, in the course of his recital, he declared in a rich rural accent: 'And then Serafina's husband died and she had his ashes cremated' ... Better – or indeed, worse – was to follow,

174

but perhaps one should first take a brief look at the *corpus delicti*, the play itself, which is, as it then was, a steamy piece of whatsa-da-matter Italian-American spaghetti opera.

Serafina is a lusty Sicilian widow who idolises the memory of her late husband. She scandalises her neighbours and the village priest by keeping his ashes (her husband's, not the priest's) in a domestic shrine, and guards her young daughter's virginity with a ferocity which would not shame, as if anything could, a Fianna Fáil deputy denouncing a dissenter.

Enter one Alvaro Mangiacavallo, a truck-driver with the body of an Adonis and the brain of a moth. He has amorous designs on Serafina, and, at one point, according to the stage directions: 'He stuffs his hands into his pants' pockets, then jerks them out again. A small cellophane-wrapped disc falls on the floor, escaping his notice, but not Serafina's.'

She rounds on him. 'You talk a sweet mouth about women. Then drop such a thing from your pocket? *Va via, vigliacco*! ... Go to the Square Roof with it ... Here is no *casa privata*. *Io, non sono puttana*!'

Thus morality triumphs and lechery is routed. The late Cornelius Jansen [Dutch Roman Catholic theologian 1585-1638] could ask for no more, but then Jansen had never been to Ireland. As recently as the late 1950s, there flourished those who believ-ed that merely to acknowledge the existence of French letters was to induce an epidemic of animalistic tumescence as far as the eye could see or the hand could grope.

This was why Simpson had been arrested, and it cut no ice that the business of dropping the vile object was merely mimed. (Indeed, if memory serves, the spectacle lingers down the years of the Pike Theatre audience rising from their seats, almost en masse, to have a gawk at the thing.) This led to the funniest moment in the entire shabby and unfunny business.

We are back in the District Court, and the prosecuting garda has reached the offending scene in the course of his résumé. An interruption comes from Counsel for the State. 'At this juncture in the play, was any object dropped on the stage?'

The good policemen thought hard and long and at last delivered himself. 'No,' he replied with some reluctance. 'Dere was nothing dropped' – then, brightening, he added: 'But it was my dishtinct impression dat it was a contraceptive dat wasn't dropped.'

The police report caused considerable argument. Defence Counsel claimed it was sympathetic and disagreement as to its being admitted led to District Justice Flynn's agreeing to 'state a case' to the High Court. The High Court decided against Simpson. Faced with enormous costs, he gambled and appealed the decision to the Supreme Court. Five judges there ruled that 'the District Justice had no legal authority to submit such a question in the first place but that he was bound to decide the matter himself'. That invalidated the High Court proceedings, so its costs were a State responsibility. Four days of the Supreme Court costs were charged to the prosecution, one to Simpson.

The taking of depositions ended in June 1958, over a year after it had begun. District Justice Flynn praised the sincerity of Gardaí but said, 'I can only infer that by arresting the accused, the object would be achieved of closing down the play. But surely if that were the object, nothing could be more devastating than to restrain the production before even a hearing is held. It smacks to me of the frontier principle, "Shoot first and talk after".' He ruled that the State had offered no evidence of Simpson's presenting an indecent performance.

Simpson was no longer at the mercy of the courts. For lack of evidence he was not returned for trial. Therefore, there could be no verdict of 'guilty' or 'not guilty'. So Irish bar-room lawyers debated. As they did, the Pike's membership dropped from 3,000 to 300. Simpson owed his lawyers money. His health suffered because of the ordeal too. But he was free, both in body and in soul, and as Tennessee Williams says, 'To be free is to have achieved your life'.

POSTSCRIPT

Theatre people are known for their ability to bounce back and for laughing in the face of adversity. About two years after the Pike production of *The Rose Tattoo*, Phyllis Ryan decided that her gallant independent company, Gemini, should produce a revival of the Williams work in a large theatre. Ryan wanted to engage as many of the original cast as possible and she even prevailed on Alan Simpson to return from France to direct. This was going to be a big, big venture.

Theatre managements were reluctant to face the possibility of renewed protests and perhaps further legal wranglings, but Miss Ryan assured them that Serafina's lover would not drop any packet of contraceptives on the stage.

Indeed, if they wished, he wouldn't even drop a paper bag or bubble gum wrapping!

For whatever reason, however, no big theatre became available and so Phyllis had to approach Dr C.S. (Todd) Andrews about producing it at the tiny Eblana Theatre, in the basement of Busáras, Dublin's main bus station. Its land-lords were Córas Iompair Éireann (Irish Transport Company) and Dr Andrews was chairman of that company. In a pragmatic fashion he told Ms Ryan that he would not expect her to tell him how to run trains, so he would not show any red signal against the up-line for *The Rose Tattoo*.

Because of limited backstage accomodation at the Eblana, Ryan had decided to dispense with the goat from the Williams' play. Simpson did not agree.

There had to be a goat! There would be no play without it! So Ryan contacted a man who lived by the canal near Leeson Street Bridge who had a goat. She persuaded him to bring the goat to a dress rehearsal. The unfortunate animal reacted in a not unusual way to the terror of its new experi-ence and stage-management complained that Equity con-tracts did not allow for mopping up after goats.

So there was another appeal to Alan Simpson. This time a raging cast and crew stood behind Phyllis Ryan as she faced the director and pointed out the difficulties. Simpson listened but refused, saying, 'It would be unlucky to drop the goat'.

'But the man keeps dropping him coming down the stairs and the goat itself seems to be forever dropping!'

The goat stayed, but after two nights the herd had had enough. He said he was tired leading his charge across the city and looking after it for long periods. Ryan thought Simpson would understand. He did not.

'Tired? What do you mean "tired"? Get him a taxi, then!' So Ryan spoke nicely to a driver who collected the goat and his handler each evening, brought them to the Eblana and drove them home after the goat's part had been played. Then this man complained about having to clean the car and about losing passengers! Gemini engaged another driver.

As the production continued, everyone except Simpson was angry with the goat. Anna Manahan, who played Serafina, was quite serious when she threatened to put it on a bus for Shercock in Co. Cavan.

So it was that at the second production of *The Rose Tattoo* in Dublin there were again protests about droppings on the stage – the goat's! This time the harsh words were all spoken backstage. And just like the first production of the play, Alan Simpson again emereged triumphant.

An unusual memorial to Simpson stands in Columb Barracks, Mullingar. As an army engineer, Simpson had designed an ornate brick hearth surround in the officers' mess ante-room there. The trouble was, it was so high that it prevented the heat from the fire spreading to the room; so his colleagues named it 'Simpson's Folly'. Many years afterwards, Eileen Colgan, Simpson's widow, performed a one-woman show in the mess. Told the story, she requested that the site of the fireplace, now long gone, be suitably marked. It now bears a brass plate that reads, 'Site of Simpson's Folly. Alan Simpson – 1920-1980'.

Alan Simpson was at the height of his career as a director when, in 1974, I worked with him on a revue staged in a provincial town. I attempted to do him a small favour. This needed the consent of two friends. That agreement was not forthcoming from either one. 'He's the fellow who was involved in *The Rose Tattoo*', one of them warned me! Ireland, Green and Chaste and Foolish had not forgotten.

More Titles from
THE COLLINS PRESS

IRISH NATURE IN FOCUS

Richard Mills and Dan Collins

A stunning collection of photographs with eloquent accompanying text illustrate the beauty and variety of the natural world in rural Ireland. Award-winning photographer with national newspaper, the *Examiner* Richard Mills, teams up with *Examiner* journalist Dan Collins to produce this quite beautiful collection, which includes studies from all sections of the natural world – flora and fauna – seals, robins, deer, cotton fields, hares, badgers, squirrels, monbretia, herons, foxes, spiders, and hedgehogs, amongst others.

paperback £14.99

FAMILY NAMES OF
COUNTY CORK

Diarmuid Ó Murchadha

This book deals with the origins of fifty of County Cork's best-known surnames and traces the early history (down to *c.* 1700) of those who bore them. Many of the families featured have never had their story related in detail before now: particulars of others are accessible only in books long out of print or in learned journals not readily available to the public. Though not a genealogical work, it should also supply a reliable foundation for those endeavouring to trace their own immediate ancestors. Each name is treated in a separate article and special attention has been given to the location of early parish seats, such as castles, parishes and townlands occupied or associated with the various families throughout the county.

paperback £11.99

A LIFETIME OF NOTES

The Memoirs of Tomás Ó Canainn

This book takes the reader on a fascinating journey through the life of the musical engineer, whose event-filled life has taken him everywhere from Belfast to Cork and Spain to Greece, learning the appropriate language en route! As a member of the well-known Cork-based traditional music band *Na Fílí*, he travelled thoughout Britain and Europe, as well as Ireland, encountering many well-known celebrities, including Brendan Behan and Clannad. In the county of Cork, where the Derry born musician now lives, he might be better known for his wranglings at University College Cork, where, as close friend of the late Sean Ó Riada, he fought with the authorities to be allowed to lecture in the Music Department, whilst already being a highly regarded lecturer in the Department of Engineering. Since retiring from his lecturing positions, he has been a well-respected music critic with the *Cork Examiner*.

paperback £7.99

DO YOU THINK YOU'LL LIKE THE WIND?

The story of a Dublin family's new life in County Clare

Paul Murphy

Born in 1957, Paul Murphy grew up in the Dublin suburb of Drimnagh. After leaving school at the age of fifteen he worked in a variety of jobs. In the 1980s he began writing and had several articles published. In 1990 Paul moved with his family to the isolated village of Kilbaha on the Loop Head peninsula in County Clare on Ireland's west coast. He is now a full-time administrator with Rural Resettlement Ireland Ltd. Of his adopted home he says: 'It is akin to Provence but without the food, the sun and the glorious houses.'

'This book is for all who have grasped at a dream and for all dreamers who believe they will too someday.'

'Paul Murphy is a writer with a story to tell and he tells it with great clarity and precision. If you live in the city and ever wondered about moving to the country, this book will make the journey for you.

If you live in the country and wondered what city folk think of you this book will give you a glimpse of yourself through city eyes.'

Alice Taylor

paperback £6.95

CAPE CLEAR: ISLAND MAGIC
A Photographic, historical and dramatic account of Clear Island, Ireland

Chuck Kruger

A convert to Cape, I'm what the locals call a 'blow-in': I've blown in from somewhere else like a seed on the wind, with the implication that I could, tomorrow, just as easily blow on to somewhere else. But I'm afraid that Cape's stuck with me, for I experience myself putting down roots into this rough sandstone island 'promontory', as it was referred to hundreds of years back. Whether I'm the toxic ragwort, the encroaching fern (bracken), the gentle Joseph's Ladder – the regional name for Monbretia – or something that hasn't grown here before and that won't upset the ecological balance, this book will make the determination clear, Cape clear.

Born in 1938, Chuck Kruger grew up in the Finger Lakes Region of New York State. In 1986 he and his wife Nell purchased a farm on Cape Clear, County Cork, where they moved in 1992. Of his adopted island he says: 'Cape's a poem I read every day, every night. It's a point of reference, a metaphor by which I confirm my very being. It's the place I love more than any other.'

paperback £6.95